SUPPLIER TO THE CONFEDERACY: S. ISAAC CAMPBELL & CO, LONDON

By

David C. Burt and Craig L. Barry

REVISED AND EXPANDED SECOND EDITION OF
MAJOR CALEB HUSE C.S.A. & S ISAAC CAMPBELL & Co

Authors OnLine
www.authorsonline.co.uk

An Authors OnLine Book

Text Copyright © David C. Burt and Craig L. Barry 2010

Cover design by Jamie Day ©

All rights reserved. No part of this publication may be reproduced, stored in a retrieval system, or transmitted in any form or by any means, electronic, mechanical, photocopy, recording or otherwise, without prior written permission of the copyright owner. Nor can it be circulated in any form of binding or cover other than that in which it is published and without similar condition including this condition being imposed on a subsequent purchaser.

British Library Cataloguing Publication Data.
A catalogue record for this book is available from the British Library

ISBN 978-07552-0623-0

Authors OnLine Ltd
19 The Cinques
Gamlingay, Sandy
Bedfordshire SG19 3NU
England

This book is also available in e-book format, details of which are available at www.authorsonline.co.uk

CONTENTS

INTRODUCTION 1

S. ISAAC, CAMPBELL & CO: THE BEGINNING 4

SHOE MAKING IN THE MID-19th CENTURY 9

WHO WAS CAMPBELL? 17

THE WEEDON BEC SCANDAL 21

SIC & Co BOUNCES BACK: SUPPLYING THE VOLUNTEERS 27

COLONEL JOSIAH GORGAS, C.S.A 31

CAPTAIN CALEB HUSE C.S.A. 35

ANDERSON, HUSE AND S. ISAAC, CAMPBELL & CO
BEGIN TO SUPPLY THE CONFEDERATE STATES 40

RUNNING THE BLOCKADE 47

THE ERLANGER LOAN 56

AGENTS PROVOCATEURS: CRENSHAW AND FERGUSON 63

GENERAL COLIN J McRAE C.S.A 73

DISPATCHING COLIN McRAE TO LONDON & THE
DELAYED ARRIVAL OF M. HILDRETH BLOODGOOD 76

THE INVESTIGATION BEGINS 83

HUSE FINALLY CLEARED 94

S. ISAAC, CAMPBELL & CO: THE END 101

CONCLUSION 108

APPENDIX A: British firms that conducted business with the Confederacy 112

APPENDIX B: Partial text of report of the investigation of Weedon Depot 117

APPENDIX C: Elliott letter 126

APPENDIX D: Alexander Collie & Co 128

APPENDIX E: Huse's British Imports 134

APPENDIX F: The Springbok 137

APPENDIX G: Northampton Shoe Factory 145

APPENDIX H: A contradiction with nothing to contradict 148

APPENDIX I: Obituaries 151

APPENDIX J: Accoutrement invoice 155

APPENDIX K: Greatcoat invoice 156

BIOGRAPHIES 157

INTRODUCTION

The Southern states seceded from the Union in early 1861 unprepared for war. They did not have the supply of arms, accoutrements, or uniforms necessary to field and equip a large standing army, and they needed all of it fast. The antebellum strategy in most of the Southern states had been to secure whatever articles were necessary (at the moment) through importation, rather than to attempt self-sufficiency by producing goods of their own manufacture. The antebellum economy in the South permitted this extravagance due to the continuing demand worldwide for cotton and tobacco. There seemed to be no reason to suspect that the future held any less promise for meeting their continuing needs, at least until the Civil War erupted. When the Federal armouries and arsenals in the Southern states fell into Confederate hands, precious few modern arms fell with them. While both sides were under-armed, the Federal armouries in the South contained mostly obsolete flintlock and smoothbore muskets of the old style and at that only about 1/3 the total numbers on hand in the North. Plans were underway by the Ordnance Department to begin the domestic manufacture of military equipment, but the realization was that attaining a level of self-sufficiency in that area was going to take time. Until then, most supplies needed to supply the armies of the Confederacy would have to be imported.

England was an important source for military equipment. To begin with, the British Government, while officially neutral and politically opposed to slavery (having made the transition to an industrial economy), was sympathetic to the Confederacy for other reasons. The British Government would not provide arms and equipment officially to the Confederacy, as the French did by supplying the Americans during the First War of Independence during the 1770s. However, the British Government made no efforts to interfere with Confederate purchases from their own commercial military industrial complexes located around London and Birmingham. In fact, up until the late 1850s with the opening of their own government arms making facility at Enfield, the British Ordnance Department contracted for all necessary equipment in much the same way. Caleb Huse arrived in London just ahead of the Federal buyers, but about ten days behind another group consisting of Francis Crowninshield and Thomas McFarland, who were on an identical mission for the Commonwealth of Massachusetts. Ironically, upon arrival they both found a buyer already in London representing the State of South Carolina. New York State also had an agent representing their interests on the ship (the *Persia*) as Crowninshield and McFarland, but unbeknownst to any of them. The London Times Illustrated on May 6, 1861 ran a notice announcing their arrival with intent to buy a quantity of military rifles which resulted in great excitement in the Gun Trade. The commercial gun-makers, sensing their present advantage in the supply/demand equation were opportunistic about their pricing, and as was noted at the time, "it does seem to me that we ought not to haggle too much…to save ten thousand dollars might be to lose everything". Consider as an example, after one Northern buyer made initial contact with John D. Goodman (Cooper & Goodman) representing the Birmingham Small Arms Trade, he learned that 25,000 P-53 Enfields were immediately available at sixty shillings each (about £3). However, before the deal could be concluded another buyer identified as representing the Confederacy stepped in with an offer of one hundred shillings each for the same lot of guns. Hence, the new price was one hundred shillings. Business was conducted this way in the Gun Quarter and the commercial gun-makers willingly facilitated the fraternal slaughter on both sides without prejudice to politics. These were the halcyon days when Birmingham gun-makers lit cigars with £5 notes. The American buyers for their part were elbowing each other out of the way to procure as many commercial military supplies as were currently available, as well as enter into new contracts for future deliveries. Complicating the tight supply, the British Volunteer movement was in full vigour, and the local civilian units contracted for (and purchased) their own uniforms and military arms. It was a very good time to be in the British Gun Trade.

Into this already crowded market on May 10, 1861, arrived Caleb Huse, just thirty years old and an Ordnance purchasing agent for the new Confederate Government. His first stop in London was to meet with Elisha Fair of Alabama, former U. S. Minister to Belgium, and from that meeting Huse satisfied himself that nothing of immediate use could be obtained from the Belgian factories. Fair told Huse that all the large houses (factories) at Liege had more contract work than they could do for several months as he had recently made direct inquiry with an eye toward obtaining arms for Alabama. In addition, the Liege gun-makers had the reputation of furnishing arms of diminished quality, hence Huse wisely decided not to give any further attention to Belgium for the present. He was, however, ready to do business on an enormous scale. To get what he needed for the Confederacy in mid-1861, Huse contracted with equipment brokers called "commission houses" that had connections in all corners of the worldwide trade. The London commission houses operated as agents for **both** the buyer and the seller exacting a fee in the form of a "percentage commission" from each. One of the biggest commission houses in London that was anxious to do business with the Confederacy was S. Isaac, Campbell & Co. Caleb Huse, lacking any better options, promptly contracted with SIC & Co, and between them began to buy and ship many of the necessary items for which the fledgling Confederacy was so desperate.

The ink was hardly dry on the first edition of David Burt's monograph about SIC & Co when Craig L Barry, author of *The Civil War Musket: A Handbook for Historical Accuracy,* contacted Burt about sharing additional research on SIC & Co as part of an upcoming Confederate research anthology. Barry also offered to help with a re-write for a possible second edition. Two heads sometimes being better than one, the material went through an extensive overhaul with each writer seeming to provide pieces of the puzzle that the other one lacked. The Trans-Atlantic partnership of two historical research writers who never met face-to-face, but shared the same intense interest in telling the same particular story, resulted in additional unpublished material; So much more material that a different title seemed appropriate to reflect the scope of the additional content.

This is the second joint effort between the two writers, the first being a booklet entitled *The Civil War Musket: J.E.Barnett & Sons.* What follows is not intended to be the final definitive history of Major Caleb Huse or S. Isaac Campbell & Co, (on the contrary) it is just the beginning of long overdue efforts to illuminate an under-researched part of a fascinating mystery, one newly titled, *Supplier to the Confederacy: S. Isaac, Campbell & Co, London.*

Craig L Barry, Murfreesboro, Tennessee
David C Burt, Congleton, Cheshire, England

S. ISAAC, CAMPBELL & CO
THE BEGINNING

Samuel Isaac
(Courtesy of Bastien Gomperts)

"Early in 1861 Saul Isaac and his nephew Benjamin Hart, both of New York City, seeing the chance of financial gain, bought out the old and established military outfitting firm of S. Campbell & Co., 71 Jermyn Street, London. Thereafter, the firm operated as S. Isaac, Campbell & Co." (1)

Virtually every word in the statement quoted in the heading is incorrect, misleading, or inaccurate. A certain lack of understanding surrounds the English firms that brokered large shipments of war materiel to the Confederacy for the first three years of the US Civil War. To begin with, the leading agent was a London commission house of army contractors doing business as S. Isaac, Campbell & Co under its managing directors, the brothers Samuel and Saul Isaac. Campbell appears to be a 'silent' or non-participating partner who will be discussed in more detail later in the monograph. Another long established myth of uncertain origin that we can debunk right out of the chute is that the S in S. Isaac, Campbell & Co stood for Saul Isaac. This is simply not the case, the 'S' is for Samuel, as the company was founded by the elder brother Samuel Isaac. Saul came to work at the firm some years after Samuel began in the military supply business.

Samuel Isaac was born in Chatham, Kent, England on November 22, 1812, to Jewish parents, Lewis Isaac (1788 –1879) a furniture broker of Poole, Dorset, and Catherine Solomon (1789 – 1863) daughter of N. Solomon of Margate, Kent. Mr Isaac senior, Samuel's father, was originally from the southwest of England and moved the family to Chatham. Young Samuel Isaac got his start in business as a "perfumer" in 1835. The mixing of scents has always required a keen sense of smell. Samuel Isaac seems to have developed his sense of smell into a good nose for money. War has always been the bedfellow of profit seekers and by 1838 he was listed as an army and navy clothier. He was successful at it and before he was thirty years old, Isaac had two homes in succession in Chatham. (2) By 1845 he was listed as a military tailor and outfitter under his own name, Samuel Isaac, at 71 High St, Chatham, Kent. Samuel was also listed in the Post Office directory for Chatham as an army contractor, military tailor and outfitter, general East India passage agent, tobacconist, trunk manufacturer, china and glass dealer, general warehouseman, and agent to Church of England Insurance trust. (3)

In 1836 Samuel's partner, Isabella Simons, gave birth to their first child, Samuel Edward Henry Isaac, who would be called Henry. In 1841, the busy entrepreneur finally married Isabella, and together they would have three more children before 1846, when she passed away at the age of 32. However, in 1848, Samuel married for the second time, to Emma Hart, daughter of Stephen Hart, and they would have two children together, Stephen Hart Isaac, and Frances Isabel Isaac. (4)

In addition to re-marrying, Samuel Isaac moved to London in 1848 where he opened his first office at 21 St James St, under the name of Isaac Samuel Army Contractor. In 1849, this changed to Isaac Samuel, Army Contractor and Outfitter, 21 St James Street, and by 1851 Samuel Isaac & Co Army Contractors, Accoutrement Makers & General East India Merchants, existed at 21 St James Street, London. In 1852 there was I.C.& Co., slightly later, "Isaac, Campbell & Co" and a C & I Isaac all had premises at High Street, Chatham. Another company, "Campbell & Co." also traded from High Street in 1858. In the census of 1851, Samuel Isaac is living at 61 Onslow Square, Kensington, London, occupation General Merchant. Finally, in 1852 there came into being the more recognised name of S. Isaac, Campbell & Co, Army Contractors of 21 St James St London, and 71 High Street Chatham.

They also kept their hand in the shoe making business with a factory in Northampton and by 1856 they are listed as providing boots and shoes to the British Royal Military Depot, or Weedon Barracks. What was the standard of quality for army boots received by the British army during the Crimean War?

"...many men have gone into hospital frostbitten, chiefly in the feet. This is probably caused, to a great extent, by the wretched manner in which the troops are shod. The only boots which they have at present are the ordinary regulation pattern, or what are called "ammunition" boots. These are made by contract, and are of inferior material, and I have heard many men complain that in the bad weather we have lately had they are completely worn out in the course of a week." (5)

S. Isaac, Campbell & Co. maintained their Northampton headquarters in Inkerman Terrace. The firm was one of several that had been providing boots to the British army in the Crimean War, such as they were. However, shoddily made army boots or not, their government contracts were suddenly cancelled following a scandal at the Weedon Bec Depot in 1858, a fiduciary matter that will also be discussed later in the monograph.

Younger brother Saul Isaac was born in Chatham, Kent, on St. Valentine's Day, 1823. He worked as a furniture manufacturer and cabinet-maker as his father was a furniture broker. In 1851, he had moved to London, and by 1854 had joined his elder brother in SIC & Co, where he was described as an Army Contractor. Saul Isaac was the financial partner of S. Isaac, Campbell & Co and headed up the soon to be infamous accounts and records of their business. (6) Keeping things in the family, on May 16, 1854, younger brother Saul married the younger Hart sister, Miriam, (Samuel had married her sister Emma in 1848) and they went on to have two children together, F.H. Isaac and Arthur Benjamin Isaac.

As was the traditional way with military outfitters of the day, the prerequisite for attracting business was a prestigious London address. According to the National Archives for Lincolnshire:

"...*On May 28, 1860 a piece of land in Pall Mall Field or Saint James Field, and the dwelling house erected thereon, known as 71 Jermyn Street, Charles Anderson Worsley Anderson Pelham, Earl of Yarborough, to Samuel Isaac, Saul Isaacs, and Charles Isaacs of 71 Jermyn Street, Army Contractors."* In addition, on September 4, 1860, *"alterations were made by Messrs Samuel Isaac, Saul Isaacs, and Charles Isaacs to the premises at 71 Jermyn Street,"* however, of what sort the archives do not specify. (7) Shortly afterwards the war between the States began. Oddly, the 1861 census for 71 Jermyn Street, London, records the inhabitants as Henry Solomans, a boarder aged 14, a clerk to army contractors, Henry Claridge, a boarder aged 18 and a clerk to army contractor, and Lionel Hart, a boarder aged 18 also a clerk to army contractors. It seems clear, however, that SIC & Co was the firm employing those clerks of army contractors at 71 Jermyn Street, and that is the address where Caleb Huse found the SIC & Co commission house in mid-May 1861, with the lengthy wish list of the Confederate Ordnance Department in hand.

NOTES:

1 Albaugh, William. *A Photographic Supplement to Confederate Swords*, Broadfoot Publishing, 1993. This same mistaken background material appears in various other collectors' guides and research anthologies. A

mistake repeated often enough unfortunately becomes accepted as the truth.
2. Children before marriage was uncommon in the Ashkenazim Jewish community in London, but not unheard of. There is one school of thought in Judaism that marriage is a duty owed to the community by those able to reproduce its members.
3. Jolles Michael, Samuel Isaac, Saul Isaac and Nathaniel Isaac Jolles Publications 1998.
4. Hopper, John. *Northamptonshire and its part in the American Civil War*, unpublished, 2006.
5. From email correspondence with William O. Adams, the quote is from a period report of a British officer labelled *Headquarters before Sevastopol, January 6th, 1855*.
6. Official records of the Union and Confederate Armies by US War Records Office, series IV vol 2 (1904) p. 890. This statement is made by Colin McRae in a letter to Gorgas on September 15th 1863.
7. National Archives, UK: Lincolnshire Archives, St Rumbold Street, Lincoln LN2 5AB, England **YARB 3/4/2/2:** —*28 May 1860, Sale of Property at 71 Jermyn Street."*

SHOE MAKING IN THE MID-19th CENTURY

As was so often the case during the Industrial Revolution, the centres of industry evolved around the sources of raw materials used in production. Birmingham was the centre for gunmaking because of the proximity to iron ore in the Midlands. Likewise, shoemaking in Britain was somewhat centred around Northampton because of the proximity to the livestock necessary for shoe leather. Since the 1820s the town had been supplying footwear throughout Great Britain, and although production was not yet mechanised, and no factories yet existed, shoe making was the major employer. (1) In fact, shoemaking was one of the largest single trades in all of England at the beginning of the 19th century, right after carpentry. By 1861 some 38% of the male population of Northampton were shoemakers, with shoes being exported as far as Australia, and the United States. In the wake of the Weedon Bec scandal, and with it the loss of their lucrative War Department contract, where better for S. Isaac, Campbell & Co to open the first modern shoe factory but in the heart of shoemaking country? (2) Well, that's the interesting part as the saying goes...

First, there was a resistance to mechanization by almost all the trades, which was something of a British populist tradition going back to the Luddites in the early part of the 19th century. Ned Ludd (it sometimes appears as Ludlam) was possibly a creation of folklore or embellished as King Ludd in homage to an actual person who reputedly broke two stocking frames with a hammer in a fit of rage in 1779, upon the introduction of looms in the British textile industry. The Luddites, taking their name from that iconic workingman's hero of a generation before, wreaked havoc on the textile industry for a while in 1811-12, even (ill-advisedly) clashing with the British army at one point. This move on the Luddites' part sent a few to the gallows and a number of others to Van Diemen's Land. (3) The widely held belief at the time was that mechanical devices separate the craftsman from the skills and dexterity which is essential to the craft. The crafts have their origins in centuries old traditions and rely heavily on honing a certain coordination of eye and hand. The Luddites saw in the industrial revolution not only a denial of their values of craftsmanship, but an end to their livelihood.

Some of the finest footwear ever made, was produced by skilled hands in the early to middle part of the nineteenth century that is *before* the wide spread use of machinery was introduced in that trade. Boots and shoes made by hand were often more durable and more attractive than anything produced since, but not faster or less expensive. Boot and shoemakers are now commonly called "cobblers." However, the word "cobbler" was then applied specifically to shoe repairmen. Those who actually hand made footwear were known as "cordwainers." (4) The London Trade Guild for this craft which includes all fine leather makers (gloves, gilders, etc) is the Worshipful Company of Cordwainers, 27th on the order of precedence of Livery Companies. (5) The cordwainers were among the last trades to be affected by the industrial revolution, as sewing machines capable of penetrating leather of the thickness used for shoe and boot uppers were not developed until the 1850s. The first machines for sewing soles and uppers were not patented until 1858, (6) but the Northampton cordwainers were not waiting until then to act.

In November 1857, the principle cordwainers held a meeting to discuss the introduction of machinery in the production of boots and shoes on the part of the Mansfield factory. The *Northampton Mercury* carried an account of the meeting, from which the following quotations are taken. At the meeting, Mr Wilder, a shoemaker, identified that the purpose of the meeting was to "Check the introduction of machinery, which was bound to bring ruin on them all."

In April 1858, the Northampton Boot and Shoemakers mutual Protection Society was formed with their stated mission "to protect raise and equalise wages." A strike fund was set up and links were coordinated with 20 principal workmen in neighbouring Stafford, who were already engaged in this dispute with their manufacturers over the same issue. Here was the new frontier of the shoe industry, a line was going to be drawn and the issue contested for both places in Northampton. Each side waited to see who would make the next move. It was not long in coming. (7)

In February 1859, twenty manufacturers of Northampton (and seventeen in Stafford) issued a statement confirming the cordwainers' worst fears: Sewing machines to close shoe uppers were coming to both cities and it was matter-of-factly announced in the following statement:

"That in consequence of sewing machines being extensively used in the cities and principal towns in the United Kingdom, so as seriously to affect the demand upon the wholesale houses any further delay in the introduction of them, by the manufacturers of Northampton, would be permanently injurious to the interest of the trade generally. And in accordance with this conviction, it was decided to introduce the machine sewn tops simultaneously into their respective trades." (8)

The reaction of the Mutual Protection Societies (Shoemakers Union) was to call a strike, urging as many shoemakers as possible to leave Northampton and seek work elsewhere, as long it was not Stafford...However, the strike proved unsuccessful and failed to rouse the ire of very many workers. It transpired that most of the Northampton shoemakers did not have any objection to the introduction of the sewing machines so long as they did not threaten any jobs. Those who did strike merely went to Leicester and took jobs on sewing machines in the factories there. After the strike had ended, and just as business returned to normal, the construction of S. Isaac, Campbell & Co's factory was completed in May 1859. This new manufactory was one of the first two completely modern shoemaking facilities in England, both of them ironically located in Northampton. (9) Samuel Isaac as a businessman had been quick to grasp that the principles of mass production were the only way forward, rather than sticking to the traditional methods of cordwainers working from their shops (and homes), hand sewing boots and shoes for delivery to the factory as they had done for generations. And there was no need for a lengthy apprenticeship, factory workers could be hired beginning at the age of nine years. With their Scrooge-like business sense and spirit of economy, about that same time the factory was ready to open, S. Isaac, Campbell & Co placed an appeal for workers in the *Northampton Mercury*, which read in part:

"To the boot and shoemakers of Northampton.

You live by work. We want work done on fair terms and for fair wages. That being so, our object is to establish those proper and just relations, which should exist between employers and the employed. We have built, at great cost, extensive premises in which to carry on the manufacture of boots and shoes.

They are arranged upon the best plan. The rooms are large, lofty, and well ventilated, and kept warmed at a uniform, moderate and healthy heat by nearly two miles of hot water piping. The engagements will be permanent for all those who are willing to do so, each day a good day's work under the superintendence of our foreman.

The work will all be piece work. The attendance must, for your sakes as well as ours, be regular. The hours fixed are – in summer from 6 to 8, from 8 1/2 to 12, and from 1 to 6 oclock; and in winter from 8 to 12, and from 1 to 4, and from 4 1/2 to 8. We intend to employ machinery. We state that plainly, because we know that many of you have striven against the introduction of machinery, but we submit to you, we are glad to know that many of you are aware of the fact, that machinery must be employed and to struggle against it is to fight with science, and an attempt to put a stop to the progress of the human mind.

We intend to employ women and children on the premises. Some of you have objected to that being done; but it is obvious that those women who work at machinery must be employed on the premises. For them separate work rooms, entrances, stair cases and personal accommodation have been provided; and they will be superintended entirely by females. Four men will work at each table. The men at each three of the tables may elect from among themselves an over-seer, who will see that the work is properly done.

We have heard your objections to what is called the factory system. We submit to you that the system that we propose is not the factory system. It is a carefully considered system of constant, orderly regulated work, without any of the bad features, which have made the factory system distasteful to you. Instead of being obliged to work in the close, confined rooms of your cottages, you will labour in healthy, commodious and well ventilated apartments. In regular hours of orderly labour, free from domestic hindrances, you will be able to do more work and earn more money in less time than you can now." (10)

Period Drawing of a Cordwainer
(Courtesy of: The Honourable Cordwainers Company)

However, the thought of the fixed hours as described therein represented an abrupt end to the traditional autonomy enjoyed by craftsmen, and it was precisely this attempt to introduce both machinery and the 'factory system' which provoked the earlier strike. In addition, the Isaacs only intended to employ non-society workers and children, meaning those who did not support the strike of 1858-59 (many did not). The sewing machines required a level of dexterity which could be learned on the job in a few months, and hence the skills of the old trade were not necessary or even desirable. The plan was of course contested by the Northamptonshire Mutual Protection Society. The *Northampton Mercury* on March 12, 1859 asked (and answered) their own question as follows:

"Is it not the factory system which is contemplated by employers more so than the machines? Yes shop-makers, it is the infernal factory system they want to introduce."

Somehow unsuccessful in this new venture, the Isaacs decided to opt out of manufacturing entirely and lease the factory out to Turner Brothers, Hyde & Co in 1861. The Isaacs eventually sold the factory outright to the Turners afterwards. (11) Ironically, Richard Turner, whose Northampton shoemaking firm was founded in the 1840s, while recognizing the economic advantages of the factory system decided not to adopt it in the 1850s for fear of antagonizing the labour force. Charles Parker, son of a boot maker himself, had run the factory when the Isaacs owned it, stayed on as general manager after Turner Brothers took over. Whatever they did differently apparently worked, because by 1862 the operation employed 300 people, and it was soon mass producing 100,000 pairs of shoes and boots per year. (12) By 1864-65 the Turner Brothers, Hyde & Co factory was exporting not only to the Confederacy, but also had huge markets in both Australia, and New Zealand.(13) Perhaps the Isaacs' failure with the shoe factory was a form of latent provincialism on the part of the Northampton workers towards Londoners, who knows? Whatever the case, SIC & Co still contracted with Turner Brothers for military footwear. Hence, a portion of the army shoes (and boots) from the same factory that SIC & Co built were later brokered by them for shipment overseas on blockade runners, destined to be worn by Confederates on the battlefields of the American Civil War. The Isaacs' Northampton shoe factory failure also serves to demonstrate the process by which the American plan of mass production or 'factory system' was adopted (grudgingly) by British workers. This was apparently the case in London as well as Northampton and Stafford as only one new firm there was recorded as utilizing sewing machines in the shoe industry before 1859. The shoemakers' strike of 1858-59 stands as the last labour strike to occur as an outright attempt to prevent mechanization.

NOTES:

1 Davenport-Hines, Richard T., *Capital, Entrepreneurs and Profit,* Frank Cass and Company (London), 1990, p. 102. Men and women worked from home, the concept of working indoors was not widely introduced until the 1890s.
2. Ibid, Davenport-Hines, p. 107. The cancelled SIC & Co government contract as a result of the Weedon Bec scandal was (in part) for army shoes, ironically enough. The Isaacs had a branch in Northampton since 1857 for the purpose of filling those contracts.
3. Van Diemen's Land was a British penal colony renamed Tasmania in 1855.
4. Rees, John F. *The Art and Mystery of a Cordwainer,* published by Gale, Curtis and Fenner, London, 1813, 140 pp. This term has its root from Cordova, the city in Spain where shoe leather was produced. Hence, one who worked with Cordovian (shoe) leather was called a cordwainer.
5. The Cordwainers controlled the leather trade back to 1272, officially recognized and chartered in 1439. The company motto is *Coriet et Arte,* which is Latin for Leather and Art.
6. The first sewing machine was designed and patented by Elias Howe in America in the 1840s and later adapted to sewing shoe uppers, which in itself revolutionized US shoe making. The shoes could be sewn inside out, dispensing with the need for a welt or an insole. A machine capable of attaching soles to uppers was patented in 1858 by Lyman Blake, another American inventor. However, soles were still pegged or hand sewn for several years afterwards though, well into the US Civil War-era, and although Federal contracts specified sewn soles, pegged bootees were accepted at a reduced rate.
7. *Mechanisation and Northampton's Shoemakers.* www.bbc.co.uk p. 3
8. Ibid, p. 3-5
9. The other new shoe manufactory belonged to Moses Philip Manfield. The term new as used here means that the firm was setting up in order to innovate and more or less completely adopt the methods of mass production.

10. Hatley, V.A., *Monsters in Campbell Square: The early history of two industrial premises in Northampton,* Northamptonshire Past and Present. Volume 4, Royal Historical Society, 1966, p 51-59.

11. Ibid, Davenport-Hines, p. 102, see footnote # 3, and also Ibid, Hatley, V.A. Two different dates are authoritatively suggested from period sources cited in these works, one cites 1863 and the other, 1872. Both dates are problematic, id est: During 1863 the shoe factory is selling enormous quantities of army shoes through SIC & Co to the CS, why would the Isaacs sell Turner the factory then? The 1872 date seems equally unlikely, but for the opposite reason…by that time both brothers had been declared bankrupt (in 1869). If Saul or Samuel Isaac had any ownership interest in a profitable shoe factory in Northampton, it would have certainly been dissolved to creditors when they liquidated. The best we can conclude is that at some point, Turner Bros took over the factory and bought it from the Isaacs, and that this same shoe factory provided an enormous quantity of army boots which were brokered by SIC & Co and purchased by the CS government.

12. Ibid, Davenport-Hines, p. 108.

13. Western Australia Business Directory 1864, Nelson Examiner and New Zealand Chronicle 1864. TBH&Co, had as its chief agent in Australia, a Mark Coronel. TBH&Co placed an advert in the New Zealand Chronicle which read in part: Turner Bros Hyde and Co having had new and extensive machinery erected for the manufacture of pegged and riveted goods. The introduction of these improvements are enabled to produce above mentioned goods of a better quality and lower prices, in much larger quantities than hitherto.

WHO WAS CAMPBELL?

It has been a subject of mystery for some time as to the identity of Campbell in the firm S. Isaac, Campbell & Co. Evidence suggests that Dugald Forbes Campbell appears to be the Campbell in S. Isaac, Campbell & Co. Dugald Forbes Campbell was born on October 19, 1814 in Glasgow, Scotland. In 1847, he was assistant manager of the Colonial Bank in London. He also translated French language books into English, and was on best terms with Prince Louis Bonaparte, III of France. Two of the works he translated were *Remarks on the Production of Precious Metals, and the Depreciation of Gold;* by Michel Chevalier in 1853, and *History of the Consulate and the Empire of France under Napoleon;* by M.A Thiers in 1851.

D. Forbes Campbell was living at 45 Dover Street, Piccadilly, London. He wrote to the Paris correspondent of the London Morning Post on January 16, 1862 about the Charleston Harbour Grievance.

"My Dear Brown:
How comes it that you have never alluded in your correspondence to the Yankee doings in Charleston harbour and the indignation threat roused in France? Upon inquiry you will find that fully three weeks ago, France and England, separately, addressed the strongest possible remonstrances to the government at Washington against the vandal like act, then in contemplation. It has been consummated in spite of our remonstrances. The foregoing I give you for a fact. I learn further from an excellent quarter, that instructions have gone to M. Mercier, to notify the Washington government that France can no longer recognize the blockade of the Southern port that the blocking up of the harbor of Charleston was uncalled for had the blockade been "effective." England approves of this and will back up France. The lead however will, on the present occasion, be taken by the Emperor. It is said too that H. M. will in his speech, on the 27th instant, denounce the barbarous mode of

warfare adopted by the North, and proclaim the blockade no longer binding on France. What joy such an announcement will occasion in Manchester and other places now sorely tried by the cotton famine?

The enclosed from the Herald of 6th inst. is the programme of the Conservative party on the American question. The party can marshal 314 men, at a division, and as 127 liberals and radicals (some of them good speakers and men of weight) are pledged to support a motion for the immediate recognition of the Confederate States and the raising of the paper blockade, the Ministry will be beaten if they do not make a virtue of a necessity and anticipate, the action of Parliament. The motion in question will be made and seconded by advanced liberals and supported by the conservatives "en masse." Make what use you like of the preceding.

Do you know whether M. Fould has determined to raise a loan? If you do, and can give me the figure and times privately by Monday morning's post, the information might put something into both our pockets. Of course you have seen Sir Robert M.P. and heard his "veni, vidi, vici." Was it he who pitched into Lord Cowley so hard, the other morning in the Times?

Yours Sincerely,
D. Forbes Campbell" (1)

In another correspondence, he denounced the choking up of the entrance of Charleston Harbor with sunken ships as barbarous; said the war was waged by the Northern states for political and territorial dominion; that the extinction or limitation of slavery with them was of an altogether secondary consideration. The U.S. Consul in Paris noted in his dispatch, the reader may expect to hear again of this Mr. Campbell. A brief analysis of all this is in order, as it lends insight into D. Forbes Campbell and his role in SIC & Co. He is the political arm of the firm. In his correspondence Campbell makes political threats he can not possibly (and will not) back up, he attempts to sway public opinion in favour of the Confederacy. For what reason would he do this? Clearly, D. Forbes Campbell hopes to profit from open shipping lanes so military supplies brokered by his firm SIC & Co can arrive unharmed at the Confederate States, particularly South Carolina.

Other events linking Campbell to SIC & Co came in a letter written by U.S.

Consul, John Bigelow. He noted in autumn 1865, *"I was the guest at a costume ball in Paris when I was presented to an English gentleman. The gentleman's name was Dugald Forbes Campbell. It appeared during the course of our interview that he was acting as an attorney for S. Isaac, Campbell & Co of London, the owners of the barque called the Springbok which had been overtaken on our coast and condemned as a blockade runner."* (2)

Still another supporting piece of evidence that makes it clear that D. Forbes Campbell was not a participating member of the firm comes from post-bellum legal documents filed on behalf of SIC & Co. to reclaim the same illegally seized *Springbok*. It reads:

"The claimants in the prize court of the cargo of the Springbok viz the firm of S. Isaac, Campbell and Co of London and Thomas Stirling Begbie also of London are the memorialists here. The firm of S. Isaac, Campbell & Co was at the time of these transactions composed of Samuel Isaac and Saul Isaac and had no other partner. The duly accredited attorney in fact of the memorialists before this commission Dugald Forbes Campbell Esq of London whose powers duly verified are filed with the Commission is not to be taken from the name of Campbell appearing in the firm of S. Isaac, Campbell & Co to have had any connection with the transactions of the voyage of the Springbok. That firm had no partner of the name of Campbell as is shown in the prize causes and in the present memorial. Mr D Forbes Campbell represents the existing interests in the claim which as is stated in the memorial are largely those of creditors of the original parties." (3)

From the known documentary evidence this much can be ascertained, it is very probable that D. Forbes Campbell received a silent partnership either via outright purchase of a partner's interest, or from the loan of a principal sum to Samuel Isaac to expand the firm in 1852. It is hardly coincidental that 1852 was when the firm changed its name from **Samuel Isaac, Army Contractors, Accoutrement Makers & General East India Merchants**, to **S. Isaac, Campbell & Co. Army Contractors of 21 St James Street London.** During this same period of time, 1852-53, D. Forbes Campbell was involved with literary translation and legal work, and hence would be unlikely to have had time for a hands-on role with the company. There is no historical record to suggest that the military supply business was of any interest to him. However, D. Forbes Campbell lists himself as agent for SIC & Co when he bought £30,000 worth of Erlanger bonds in 1863. Forbes is there in the picture, but always at arm's length. Yet who better to have as an agent or silent partner in SIC & Co than a barrister of high status, influence, and wealth, especially when you are seeking to secure military supply contracts with the British Military? D. Forbes Campbell died in 1886 ironically, the same year that his partner Samuel Isaac passed on.

NOTES:

1. Bigelow, John, *Retrospections of an Active Life*, Baker & Taylor, 1909, p. 449.
2. Bigelow, John, *Gladstone, Morley and the Confederate Loan of 1863*. Published DeVinne Press, London, 1905. See Note 1: *"The firm consisted of Samuel and Saul Isaac, though Moses Brothers had a beneficial interest in the cargo."*
3. Evarts, William Maxwell, *Arguments and Speeches of William Maxwell Evarts*, Macmillan Company, 1919, p. 693. See also: *Sessional Papers of the House of Commons, Correspondence respecting the Seizure of the British Vessels Springbok and "Peterhof" by United States Cruisers in 1863*, Miscl. No. I (1900), C. 34][Sessional Papers of the House of Commons, p.39.

Picture of Weedon Bec Magazine
(Courtesy of Subterannea Britannica)

THE WEEDON BEC SCANDAL

On February 1, 1856, the Jewish Chronicle (London) reported the following:

"The contract for the supply of clothing to the whole of the British Army in the East has been taken by Messrs Isaacs, the Army contractor of Chatham and St James St London. It is anticipated that this firm will also have the contract for providing clothing and regimental necessaries to the whole of the Army, the Government having decided on placing a contract in the hands of one contractor only."

In addition, on May1st, 1858 SIC & Co won another major contract for the supply of "Regulation Boots". (1) During the Napoleonic Wars, the British military adopted the laced ankle height Blucher boots, rather than the previous buckled variety. These were somewhat similar to the US produced Jefferson Bootee except with two brass eyelets per side and a twill pull loop on the spine. (2)

This was a major coup for SIC & Co as the British army was active in India putting down the Indian Sepoy mutiny of 1857-58. However, in June 1858 the SIC & Co lost their government contract with the British Regular Army following reports of bribery and corruption at the Military storehouse at Weedon Bec in Northamptonshire. The Royal Military Depot, as it became known, opened in 1803 and stretched out along the Nene valley above the village of Lower Weedon in Northamptonshire, with a barracks for 500 men overlooking the Depot to the north, close to the Coventry road. The Depot became the main clothing and general stores for the British army and initially the depot had eight storehouses and four magazines. The storehouses were of brick construction and faced with stone, each of two storeys and 160 feet long by 35 feet wide, divided into four rooms. One of the buildings was converted into a military prison with three stories that contained 121 cells. The adjoining building was used as the hospital and one of the adjacent buildings housed a chapel. The eight buildings covered a distance of approximately a quarter of a mile with the magazine buildings some three hundred yards to the west in a separate walled enclosure. The Depot was used for storage and issue of small arms and ordnance as early as 1809.

In order to move goods quickly into the Depot, a tributary cut from the nearby Grand Junction canal was constructed between the two rows of storehouses. At each end of the main enclosure, two lodges were built over the canal, each equipped with a movable portcullis. Cupolas surmounted each the lodges and that on the east lodge a clock that still chimes and keeps perfect time to this day. The canal cut continued into the magazine passing through a further smaller building and portcullis. At the western end there is a forth portcullis leading to a barge turning area outside the perimeter wall. Barges were also able to turn in a canal basin within the magazine enclosure.

Gunpowder was delivered to Weedon by barge, where it was packed into barrels and boxes and re-issued. The coming of the railway bought a standard gauge rail link to the depot. (3)

James Elliott was the principal storekeeper at the Weedon Bec Depot, having previously been in the Ordnance Department in London. He was appointed on a commission to inquire into the military expenditure in Canada from 1837-39, and in 1845 was promoted to chief clerk at headquarters in Canada. In 1851, he was appointed a member of the commission to inquire into the naval and military establishments abroad; and in 1855 received the appointment of chief superintendent of military stores at the Weedon Bec Depot. By December 1857, Elliott was suspected of irregularities in his accounts at Weedon, and the Government was determined to remove him to Ireland. Elliott was discharged from service, but was retained at Weedon for purposes of balancing his cash and stock books, and remained until May 1858, when he defenestrated to America with his mistress to avoid prosecution.

The difficulties arose when James Elliott received from the government £1,500, with which to pay up an account due, and £200 to pay another account due to the Grand Junction Canal Co. These monies he appropriated to his own purposes, and thereby involved himself so seriously in difficulty as to be unable to meet additional accounts including wages due to be paid at the

Weedon Bec Depot. He applied to the War Department for money to cover the wages for the month of May, but was refused, and by May 14, was unable to pay anyone. Samuel Isaac (SIC & Co) was at the Weedon Bec a few days later and was called on by Elliott. James Elliott asked Samuel Isaac for a loan of £500 for three days, Isaac agreed without enquiry or for what purpose it was wanted. (4) The money was paid into the Northampton Bank on May 16, and the following Monday Elliott gave a cheque to one of the clerks at the depot to cover the wages. The money given by Samuel Isaac was still not sufficient and another £350 was obtained from Cox & Co, a firm commonly called the 'Bankers of the British Army.' However, Cox & Co were also the official brokers for the sale and purchase of Military Commissions, the recognised intermediaries for regimental exchanges and transfers; and the executive agents for the supply work involved in the clothing and equipment of the British army. (5) James Elliott, with the funds from Cox & Co in his pocket, embarked for Liverpool, and then headed for America. In addition, the War Department discovered that Samuel Isaac had paid a cheque into Elliott's bank account.

On November 19, 1858, Samuel Isaac was summoned to appear before a Royal Commission charged with enquiring into the state of the store and clothing depots at Weedon Bec Depot. Worse still, on top of the loan to Elliott, Isaac stood accused of altering contracts for regulation boots at the depot. The plan was for SIC & Co boots and shoes to be sent into the depot, and then declared surplus sales so Isaac could buy the articles back at knock down prices.

When asked why Isaac had loaned the storekeeper £500 (6) Isaac said that he made the loan to a friend, having been told by Elliott there was not enough money to pay wages due, and it was a loan for three days only.

Indeed Elliott himself wrote to Samuel Isaac from his new home in New York offering to back up his claim that the money lent was indeed nothing but a loan. This letter was read out to the commission. It stated (in part):

"Dear Sir – Having read in the papers a statement referring to the loan of £500 made by you to me, and to various public dealings with you as a contractor, which statement, if explained, might give to these transactions character not in accordance with the facts, I think it right, both in justice to

myself and to you, to say that, as to the £500 having been given as a bribe, or for any favours shown to you in the discharge of my public duties, the assertion is a cowardly and calamitous falsehood, which no man, however high his position, would dare to advance were I in England".

The letter concluded:

"I may add that I am ready at any moment to declare, on oath, that the loan of £500 was the first and only private monetary transaction of any description between us, which, at the time of borrowing, I was fully persuaded it would have been in my power to replace out of money that I then had a prospect of raising." (7) (See Appendix C)

As a result of this and because of failings at Weedon Bec Depot in recording actual transactions by their own clerks, plus key witnesses being unable to provide any clear evidence that proved any charges, the investigating committee failed to *prove* malfeasance against SIC& Co, or Samuel Isaac individually. However the loan was seen as an improper gratuity which was technically a breach of contract. Consequently, the SIC & Co contracts were cancelled immediately, and they were banned from any future contracts with the War Department. (8)

In a letter dated June 30, 1858 from the War Office read:

"Sirs, you are required to take notice that I hereby determine the contract bearing date the 1st May 1858, for supply of army regulation boots, at the end or expiration of three months, following this month in which the notice is given."

Another letter enclosed stated:

"Sirs, I am directed by Major Gen Peel to transmit a notice to you terminating your contract of the 1st May 1858, for the supply of army regulation boots." (9)

It seems the War Department was considerably less incensed with Cox & Co than with SIC & Co over their respective loan(s) to Elliott. Was this some form of anti-Semitism? Not at all, it appears that the real issue was not the loan to Elliott prima facie, but rather the discovery of the Isaacs' attempted surplus buy back shenanigans, which although not proven were still believed to be the truth of the matter. The loss of their War Department contract came as a shock to Samuel Isaac, who over the course of the next year lobbied several times and requested re-instatement, all in vain. The British War Department was prickly towards any future business with the Isaacs — "once bitten, twice shy" as the saying goes. The SIC & Co firm got around the ban by supplying some of the new Volunteer Companies of the British army formed in 1859 and comprised of citizen soldiers who purchased all their own equipment, including uniforms. This was a sizeable new market for military supplies, though. The French were making belligerent threats and the British army was spread thin at the time. As a result, when the Volunteers were called, 160,000 civilian men sought to equip themselves all about the same time, and there were no War Department auditors to run a fine toothed comb through any of these contracts. If nothing else, the Volunteer sales kept the wolf away from the door of the SIC & Co commission house until Caleb Huse came calling a couple years later. (10)

NOTES:

1. Jolles, Michael, *Samuel Isaac, Saul Isaac and Nathaniel Isaac,* Jolles Publications, 1998, 309 pp.
2. Jefferson Bootees were so-named for Thomas Jefferson, not Jefferson Davis despite whatever nonsense you might read to the contrary. They were named in homage to Thomas Jefferson who wore laced shoes to his inauguration instead of the then common buckled shoes.
3. Hopper, John, *Northamptonshire, and its part in the American Civil War*, unpublished, 2006.
4. Doubtful, but this is what Samuel Isaac testified before the commission looking into the Weedon Bec matter. This would not have been in character.
5. Cox and Co began in 1758 when founder Richard Cox was appointed as regimental agent of the Grenadier Guards. The Company is still doing business as Cox & Kings. See: *Cox's & King's: The Evolution of a Military Tradition.*
6. About £22,000 or $31,400 (US) in today's money.
7 Times Newspaper Archive. Royal Commission of Army Contracts, Times Newspaper, November 1858.

8.Correspondence with Michael Jolles
9.Ibid, Jolles.
10.The French were doing what they do when they run out of imagination that is threatening an ill-advised invasion of Britain. Cooler heads ultimately prevailed, which was fortunate for the French.

Picture of Weedon Bec Clothing Depot
(Courtesy of Subterranea Britannica)

SIC & Co BOUNCES BACK: SUPPLYING THE VOLUNTEERS

After losing their contract with the War Department, the ever-opportunistic SIC & Co got around the ban in 1859 by instead supplying the newly formed Volunteer regiments. What was the Volunteer movement in Britain about? The original British Volunteer units formed during the Napoleonic-era with the stated purpose of defending the homeland from the French, which had forces massing on the coast near Boulogne. These Volunteers were strictly temporary, raised in a hurry to meet that specific threat, and never part of the regular British army forces. For example, a Volunteer's idea of military duty would not include being shipped out to fight overseas, but rather it was limited to the defence of England at home in the event of invasion. All in all, over 460,000 Volunteers availed themselves from 1794 to 1814, but after the French defeat by the British navy at Trafalgar they were never needed and eventually the Volunteer units dissipated afterwards, when their uniforms began wearing out.

However, on the heels of the Crimean War of the mid-1850s (with Russia), and the Sepoy Rebellion in India a few years later, the British army was spread thin across the empire. Less than a third of all effectives remained in England, a number sufficient for peacetime but when an assassination attempt in 1858 on the French King Napoleon II was linked to a bomb made in England, there were rumours of a knee jerk invasion of "perfidious Albion" in retribution by the French. (1) The British civilian population was alarmed and demanded arms to assist in resistance. This was called the Panic of 1859 and from this little flare-up the 2nd Volunteer Movement resulted, beginning the same year. Fortunately for the militarily disaster-prone French, they restrained their *elan* after imbibing their daily evening intake of *la fee verte* and wisely did not invade England. (2) The British civilian men, however, were keen on the idea and took hold of the opportunity to keep arms, a right we take for granted as constitutionally protected in America, but a thing unknown in other parts of the world. It became a fad, and by 1861 there were more than 170,000 British volunteers organized into units often named for the county where the men lived, i.e.; The 4th Herefordshire Volunteer Rifle Corps which was raised in April, 1860 or the Shropshire Volunteer Rifle Corps. Of these Volunteer units, the vast majority (135,000) of men were in rifle or light infantry companies. Some Volunteer units did eventually see action in the *fin de siècle* Boer War, but were using much more modern weapons by that time. (3)

Despite regular drill and target practice by Volunteer units, the regulars in the British army somewhat looked down upon the Volunteers at best, as parade fodder and at worst, largely worthless. They were lampooned in cartoons depicting a festively plump man in a gaudy uniform under the title John Bull Guards his Pudding. The Volunteers were also chastised in song and the following ditty (which seems along the lines of Goober Peas) comes from the British magazine **Punch**:

"Some prate of patriotism, and some of cheap defence,
But to the high official mind that's all absurd pretence,
For all the joys of snubbing, there's none to it so dear,
As to snub, snub, snub, snub the British Volunteer..." (4)

Of course, the Volunteers paid out-of-pocket to arm themselves and both the Isaac brothers were Officers in the Rifle Volunteers. Samuel Isaac was commissioned a Captain Commandant of the 5th Northamptonshire 1-A Battalion Rifle Volunteers on March 3, 1860, and was promoted to Major on July 24, 1868. Saul Isaac was made Captain of the 46th Westminster Rifles. (5) The images of British Volunteers from the US Civil War-era are sometimes misidentified as Confederates with British accoutrements. (6) The men in the Northampton Volunteers were mostly workers from the Isaacs' former shoe factory in Northampton, with the Officer Corps of the new Battalion made up from men of the most prominent families in Northamptonshire. These Volunteer companies of 80 men each drilled several times per week after work. The Isaacs' personal involvement with the Volunteer companies made SIC & Co well placed to equip these (and other) outfits. The equipment used by the Volunteers did not have to conform to regular War Department regulations. And therefore none of the Volunteer kits produced or brokered by the company needed to pass any rigorous government inspection process, nor did it have to be tested in battlefield conditions. SIC & Co marked Volunteer kits have been identified with Confederate provenance as well as some received in September 1861, by the Commonwealth of Massachusetts.

Equipage and cloth provided for the Confederate States Government at inflated prices by SIC & Co, as Major James B. Ferguson was to discover, was of substandard craftsmanship, made with the lowest quality leather, with sloppy stitching, and poor construction. Further evidence of the firm selling shoddy goods comes from a report in 1858, which stated:

"With regard to knapsacks, some supplied by Isaac were of inferior quality, the canvas being rough, and the corners not being waterproof.
There was also confusion over the name Messrs Isaac & Campbell being marked on them; there had been confusion over whether the knapsacks which had failed a test in which samples were compared against a sealed pattern, were genuinely from the same supplier as that of the sealed sample." (7)

But as the fledgling Confederate Government prepared for war, Europe and particularly Great Britain seemed the ideal places to secure lacking and much needed war material. Anything being better than nothing, quality needed to be serviceable, but wasn't the entire issue –quantity was. And poor quality military goods were not limited to CS imports from SIC & Co, bloodshed has historically been found to mix well with the prosperity of opportunists. Shoddy goods were certainly an issue faced by the Federal Quartermaster, a department famously cheated by Northern profiteers early in the American Civil War. (8) Military supply appears to have always been a racket.

The sales to Volunteer units enabled SIC & Co to stay in business until Caleb Huse came calling in mid-May, 1861.

NOTES:

1. As things turned out (except for Napoleon), nobody in Europe had anything to worry about from the French military since the time of

Charlemagne (at least after his 778 debacle at Roncevalles) on through to the present day.

2. *La fee verte*, the Green Fairy meaning Absinthe...a concoction distilled from wormwood that is a potent 80% alcohol. Instead of happy hour, the French enjoyed their daily green hour where they swilled absinthe in their little sidewalk cafes until they were in a stupor.

3. Fin de siècle or turn of the century, this generally refers to the end of the 19th and beginning of the 20th. The South African Boer War was 1899 to 1902.

4. *Punch* magazine, August 20, 1887. *Punch or The London Charivari*, later *Punch* was a Fleet Street published weekly magazine that ran from 1841 to 2002, specializing in cartoons and satire.

5. Jewish Chronicle, April 6, 1860. Note: You could not hold a commission in the British army if you were Jewish until 1858. Source: author's discussions with John Hopper (various dates).

6. The picture on page 17 of Albaugh's More Confederate Faces (Broadfoot Publishing 1993) identified as a Confederate soldier, is actually a British Volunteer.

7. Jolles, Michael, *Samuel Isaac, Saul Isaac and Nathaniel Isaacs* (self published, London 1998).

8. Antebellum, almost all US army shoes were produced at Susquehanna Arsenal. The leather sections were cut out in the Arsenal and then "farmed-out" to independent workers who put them together in their home/shops on a piecework basis, much as they did in Northampton at the same time period. That system of manufacture changed quickly with the need for mass produced army shoes in mid-1861. Factories sprung up in response to the newly available US Government contract work. One New York factory contracted to produce 120,000 pairs of army shoes. How good were they? The US Congressional Hearings of 1862 was formed to investigate sub-standard supplies provided by contractors to the Union army. During one, a shoe manufacturer was called to testify that had apparently produced army boots with paper under very thin leather soles. The boots literally fell apart almost immediately after a few infantry marches. According to the Official Record of the 37th Congress, Session 2, p. 1569, when confronted with these allegations the contractor replied, "but those boots were supposed to go to the Cavalry."

COLONEL JOSIAH GORGAS, C.S.A

Josiah Gorgas C.S.A.

The man chosen by the Confederacy to lead the new CS Ordnance Department was, like Caleb Huse, a Northerner. Josiah Gorgas was born in Running Pumps, Pennsylvania on July 1, 1818, one of ten children. His father, Joseph Gorgas was at various times employed as a farmer, clockmaker, mechanic and innkeeper. Because theirs was such a large family, the elder Gorgas and his wife struggled at times to provide for all their needs. Hence, Josiah did not have much opportunity for formal education. There was certainly nothing in his family background that suggested that Gorgas was an administrative wizard who would contribute more except perhaps for one man (1) to the success of the Confederate armies. One distinguishing physical feature staring back from the surviving photographs of his profile is the slightly crooked nose of a pugilist. However, it was not broken due to a punch from an adversary, but rather Josiah broke his nose when he tripped and fell at age three. (2) There must not have been a physician available to set the break based on the photographic evidence.

When he was age seventeen, he left home to live with an older, married sister in Lyons, New York, where he found a job in the office of a newspaper printer. (3) He was diligent about his work and came to the attention of the company lawyer, Graham Chapin, who was also their local Congressman. Chapin took on the young man to study law in his own offices. Chapin had the connections to get Gorgas in to West Point, where he graduated 6th in the class of 1841. The army assigned Gorgas to the Ordnance Department where he served under General Winfield Scott in the Mexican War. After the war ended, while serving at Mt Vernon in Alabama, he met and married Amelia Gayle, the daughter of the former Governor of Alabama, John Gayle. They had six children. The Gorgas family was living in Philadelphia when the first Southern states seceded in the winter of 1860–61. Josiah mulled over, but ultimately declined a commission in the Confederate Army in February, but when he learned of a pending transfer from his duties at Frankford Arsenal to foundry duty under Benjamin Huger, he resigned from the U.S. army effective April 3, 1861. General Pierre G T Beauregard recommended Gorgas to Jefferson Davis and he accepted the second Confederate offer for the rank of Major of Artillery. After another officer declined the position, he became chief of the new Confederate Bureau of Ordnance on April 8, 1861.

At the time Josiah Gorgas took over the Confederate Ordnance Department, the Southern states were without any means to produce sufficient military arms, ammunition or powder. This problem was compounded since the United States War Department years before the war reduced the supplies in the Arsenals located in the Southern states to a fraction of what was on hand in the North. (4) It was clear that Gorgas inherited a house in disarray and having nothing on hand to work with the supply bureaus had nothing to issue. In addition, there were limited funds available for purchasing imported military wares. (5) Until building the necessary infrastructure and securing machinery for the production of military supplies, Gorgas had to organize a provisional operation to meet the immediate needs of the Confederacy.

One of his primary tasks was to select a purchasing agent to Europe to obtain arms and munitions for the government. The individual Gorgas selected for this critical mission was Caleb Huse, a man in whom Gorgas had total confidence. As matters would unfold, that confidence in Huse as well as his own judgment was soon going to be put to the test. (6) Caleb Huse left American soil undercover to travel half-a-world away to London with nothing more than £10,000 in the form of a letter of credit from Fraser, Trenholm & Company. With that small sum, Huse was to obtain a list of needed items for the new nation as long as his coat sleeve. Of course, purchasing agents much like the governments they serve, always needed money. After arriving in London, Huse soon found the Isaacs who were outspoken in their desire to serve the South. As a result, Huse would continue to need substantial amounts of money for some time to come. (7)

Reading between the lines, a portrait of Josiah Gorgas emerges as an officer who at times struggled to work effectively with his superiors. His relationship with his commander (Colonel H.K. Craig) in the US Ordnance Department was adversarial. His relationship with the Confederate Secretary of War, James A. Seddon, was not much better. It was only for his results; that is to say Gorgas' success building from nothing a Confederate War industry, and his success blockade running needed goods into the country that Seddon did not take action against him.

Notes:

1. The exception would (of course) be Robert E. Lee. Feel free to disagree if you like, the fact is that while the Confederate Army often lacked enough

food, and their supply system was chaotic, they never lacked for arms and ammunition. According to his biographer, The world has hardly seen such a transformation of ploughshares into swords.
2. Vandiver, Frank E. *Ploughshares into Swords: Josiah Gorgas and Confederate Ordnance.* Austin, TX: University of Texas Press, 1952. pp. 3-8. Much of the biographical information comes from the diary of Josiah's brother, Solomon Gorgas.
3. Wiggins, Sarah Woolfolk, ed. *The Journals of Josiah Gorgas, 1857–1878.* Tuscaloosa, AL: University of Alabama Press, 1995.
4. The ORs, series 3, volume 1, show the number of serviceable muskets on hand in each of the arsenals before 1861. Despite Secretary of War Floyd's efforts to stockpile a few more modern weapons in the South, the Northern arsenals not only outnumbered those in the South, but held 3 times the numbers of weapons. The Southern arsenals did have the higher numbers of flintlock muskets from before the Mexican War, though.
5. Ibid, Vandiver, p.58
6. Ibid, Vandiver, p. 61
7. Ibid, Vandiver, pp. 83-87.

CAPTAIN CALEB HUSE C.S.A.

Caleb Huse C.S.A.

Passing through New York in disguise and sending his baggage by another route, Caleb Huse arrived in Liverpool on May 10, 1861. Upon landing he quickly travelled to London to be nearer the Capital's vast armament industries. Huse had graduated from West Point in 1851, and later served as an instructor of Chemistry there. He took a leave of absence of one year in 1859 to travel to London, Vienna and Paris, *"...with a view of presenting the James projectile to those...governments."* (1)

The James projectile was a 14 lb. artillery shell patented by Charles Tillinghast in 1856. It had the undesirable characteristic of losing its lead sabot in mid-flight, normally while over friendly troops, an inconvenience which was deemed unacceptable. In 1860, Huse was granted another leave of absence to serve as Superintendent and Commandant of Cadets at the University of Alabama. (2) This was a thinly veiled endeavour by the state of Alabama to have potential officers trained in the likely event of secession. For their part, the Cadets considered Huse *"nothing but a d-----d Yankee"* and they planned a small mutiny but the state of Alabama seceded before the cadets could, and Huse was off on his way to London. (3)

Huse hailed from Newburyport, Massachusetts. His Yankee roots immediately aroused suspicion in the new CS Government, just as they had a year earlier in Alabama and likely the distrust of many Southern born Confederates. There was a good deal of provincialism on both sides in those days. The Union was particularly disappointed with Huse as well, not only for accepting a Confederate commission, but the manner in which he did so. Huse only resigned his commission as Lieutenant of Artillery in the Union army in May 1861, after being commissioned a Captain in the Confederate States Army a month prior in April. His resignation was backdated to February 25, 1861. (4) Additionally, the thinking of the time was that a native born Southron could be excused for sympathizing with their State first over the Federal authority, as was the case with Robert E. Lee. However, Huse was excoriated in the Northern press as a traitor who *"...abandoned his State, Country, principles and friends to engage in the business of furnishing supplies to the rebels..."* (5)

After arriving in London, Huse rented a flat at 58 Jermyn Street; located directly across the street from his flat were the offices of S. Isaac, Campbell & Co, whom, until recently had been a shoe contractor for the British army.

(6) Huse was observed *"to be living in splendid style in London on the fraudulent funds...of the Rebel Government."* (7)

Huse made prompt contact with the firm, and the Isaacs were glad for the opportunity to outfit the Confederate armies. SIC & Co brokered all the goods needed from various sources, and charged a commission for their service. This arrangement was convenient for Huse, as it meant he didn't have to invest valuable time seeking out all the Ordnance Department war materiel on his own in a foreign country.

However, because of his Yankee heritage and suspicious of his possible motives, Confederate President Jefferson Davis summoned Major Edward C. Anderson and was told by Davis that as a consequence of his Northern roots and certain letters written by Huse from Canada the Government had reason to mistrust Huse. As a result Anderson was to proceed to England to work along side him and to examine his conduct and to replace him if he was found to be any way disloyal.

Then Secretary of War, Leroy Pope Walker, in writing to Anderson on May 18th, 1861 declared that:

"You are hereby authorized, should circumstances in your opinion demand it, to supersede Capt Caleb Huse, who was sent to Europe as an agent of this Department to purchase ordnance, arms and munitions of war, and to take possession of any assets or credits placed to his account as such agent". (8)

Anderson arrived in England in June 1861, and started to work along side Huse in the purchase of war materiel. He found Huse to be completely competent and loyal to the Confederate cause and wrote on July 17th, 1861:
"My first duty on my arrival in England was to comply with the instructions which I had received in Montgomery and to scrutinize very closely the operations & sentiments of Capt Huse. To this end I conferred very fully with Mr Prioleau, our financial agent, & more particularly with Captain Bulloch, whose closer intimacy with H would enable him to afford me correct information. From both I received the most satisfactory assurances of the fidelity & loyalty of Mr H-.My own intercourse confirmed this, and I took the earliest opportunity to relieve the minds of the Confederate authorities of the apprehensions which Huse's thoughtless letter, written

from Canada on his way over, had excited, and upon which I had been sent to England to control him." (9)

Satisfied everything was in good hands with Huse, Anderson would continue to work with him and go on to purchase the iron-hulled, propeller driven steamship *Fingal,* which made its maiden voyage to Savannah with him on board. It landed safely on November 12, 1861, and neither one returned to England. Major Anderson remained to assist with the defence of Savannah, and the *Fingal* was refitted into an ironclad warship. (10)

NOTES:

1. The Cadet School was created at Tuscaloosa, where the University of Alabama was founded in 1818. All but seven buildings were burned when Union troops occupied the university in 1865, including the library. Both books in their literary accumulation were lost and more tragically one had not even been colored in with crayons yet.
2. *A Rebel Diplomat: A Sketch of Caleb Huse*, NY Times, April 10, 1864. Huse stayed in Jermyn Street until July 1862, when he moved to 38 Clarendon Road Notting Hill, London. He received much of his correspondence at the offices of SIC & Co, at 71 Jermyn Street.
3. Huse, Caleb, *The Supplies for the Confederate Army*, Boston: T.R. Marvin & Son Press, 1904, p. 6-9.
4. Ibid, Huse, p. 8. His own account soft soaps this particular point, but Huse was technically on leave of absence from the US army until May 1861, by which time he was a CS purchasing agent in London buying ordnance supplies from SIC & Co. As far as his rank, Huse claims "Jefferson Davis greeted me as *Major* Huse before he departed for England". However, he later states "I had been advanced to the grade of Major" after he discusses the capture of the *Stephen Hart* (p. 29) which was caught running the blockade on January 29, 1862…but at any rate soon after arriving in England he was elevated in rank to Major. He was referred to as Captain Huse when he called on London Armoury the day after arriving in London.
5. Ibid, NY Times
6. The British army found the boots from SIC & Co to be substandard, and the infantry in the Crimea reported their shoes wearing out in a week. This however was not the reason the contract was cancelled.

7. Ibid, NY Times
8. OR Series IV Volume I p332-333
9. Hoole SW, *Confederate Foreign Agent, The European Diary of Major Edward C. Anderson.* Confederate Publishing Co 1976. p 31 The first Confederate Capital was in Montgomery, Alabama.
10. McNeil, Jim, *Master of the Shoals*, DaCapo Press, 2003, p. 38.

ANDERSON, HUSE AND S. ISAAC, CAMPBELL & CO BEGIN TO SUPPLY THE CONFEDERATE STATES

On June 27, 1861, just a few days after his arrival in London, Major E. C. Anderson accompanied Caleb Huse to the establishment of Messrs S. Isaac, Campbell & Co where they ordered 2,000 sets of accoutrements for the Confederate Government. And on August 3, Anderson reported, *"Wrote to S. Isaac, Campbell & Co and ordered an additional number of sabres so as to number 1,000."* On August 22, 1861, Anderson again wrote *"Bought from Isaacs 10,000 muskets old pattern"*, and the following day *"Contracted with Isaacs for a lot of (P53) Enfields and for 11,000 English muskets of very good quality."* (1) During these halcyon days of mid-1861 Anderson and Huse are like the proverbial 'kids in a candy store' and their correspondence here reflects that they can barely contain their enthusiasm.

On August 27, 1861, Samuel Isaac sent a telegram to Major Anderson, who was at Dover in Kent, informing him of good news. SIC & Co had secured a contract with *Behrings* Bros & Co, (sic) (Barings) who had previously been supplying the US Government, for 4,000 Enfield rifles per month for the next six months. (2) The United States agents having run out of funds and were being made to forfeit some £5,000 deposited as a guarantee. This was fortuitous not only because it served the needs of the Confederacy but had the additional advantage of keeping these arms from being used against them in America by the invading Union army. As a gesture of appreciation to Samuel Isaac for all the valuable work he had done, Anderson promised him his influence with the Confederate Government in *"obtaining for him the appointment of Consul General in England in the event of the success of our cause."* (3) The Jefferson Davis government in Richmond was also delighted by the involvement of SIC & Co in the Confederate war effort, so much so that the acting Secretary of War, Attorney General Judah P. Benjamin wrote to the Isaacs' firm on March 17, 1862, thanking them as follows:

"Gentlemen: I am in receipt of your favor of January 29th by the Economist, and desire to express to you the deep sense of obligation felt by this Government for the kind and generous confidence you have shown in us when other foreign countries seem to be doubtful, timorous, and wavering. You will find, however, that your confidence was not misplaced, and that we have not failed (as far as we could find means) to make remittances to Capt Huse, although not as rapidly as desired; but our difficulties have been great in procuring secure remittances. Enough has been done however, we trust to relieve you from embarrassment or apprehensions. I find from my books that the amounts furnished to Capt Huse have been recently as follows
From Jan 20th 1862 to March 7th 1862 $1,261,000.

Our demands from England will continue to be quite large, and we trust you may find your connection with our young Government equally profitable and agreeable." (4)

Things were off to a good start. This meant Huse could not only service some of the Confederate debts to SIC & Co, but aggressively carry on lining up future purchases. By the end of 1862, Huse had contracted for over £1,000,000 ($5,000,000 Confederate) worth of military supplies mostly through S. Isaac, Campbell & Co. Much of this was on credit advanced by the Isaacs' firm themselves with about half of this amount still unpaid. Military items shipped to the Confederacy included the non-standard British Volunteer type accoutrement set, which consisted of belts (snake-hook and other), the P-1845 sling mounted cap pockets, (cap pouch), cartridge pouches (cartridge boxes), hard frame and other knapsacks with mess tins and mess tin covers, close to 185,000 P-1853 Enfield long rifles, additional P-1856 short rifles, P-1861 ball bags, frogs and bayonet scabbards, slings, oil bottles, and a multitude of other military items, even some woollen Confederate battle flags. (See appendix E)

After Anderson departed aboard the *Fingal,* perhaps a bit recklessly, Huse began buying large amounts of goods not only for the Ordnance Department, but for the Quartermaster and Commissary Department(s) as well. The purchases included: wool greatcoats, large quantities of wool cloth, army boots, trousers and socks. Samuel Isaac also presented Huse with a deal to buy British army surplus items for the Quartermaster Department, like shirts and blankets. These purchases were outside of his original orders, which included the purchase of small arms and munitions only. Since no attempted good deed goes unpunished, the decision to go beyond the designated role of ordnance purchasing agent would have unseen future consequences for Huse. However, Josiah Gorgas continued to be delighted with his efforts, and wrote to the new Secretary of War, James A. Seddon on December 5, 1862:

"The purchase of ordnance stores in foreign markets on Government accounts are made by Maj Caleb Huse, C.S. Artillery, who resides in London, and whose address is No 38 Clarendon Road, Notting Hill, West London. Major Huse was detailed for this duty in April 1861. His instructions directed his attention chiefly to the purchase of small arms, but his list embraced all the necessary supplies. Under those instructions he has purchased arms to the number of 157,000 and large quantities of gunpowder, some artillery, infantry equipments, harness, swords, percussion caps, saltpetre, lead, & c. In addition to ordnance stores, using rare forecast, he has purchased and shipped large supplies of clothing, blankets, cloth, and shoes for the Quartermasters Department without special orders to do so." (5)

The American Civil War came at just the right time for the commission house of SIC & Co. The firm had recently lost their British army contracts, and with it their major revenue stream. SIC & Co had provided large amounts of clothing and equipage for the British army during the Crimean War, as well as during the Sepoy Rebellion in India, and they were anxious to do the same for the Confederacy. What was a commission house and how did it work? The role of a commission house was as follows: A wishes to import goods from B but has no money. B does not know A as they are not yet an established or officially recognized foreign government which limits their recourse… ipso facto, credit is out of the question. The commission house steps in as an intermediary, finds and contracts for the goods from multiple parties and often buying in bulk directly from manufacturers. They then arrange credit or financing. For providing these services the commission house charges a fee of 2 to 2 ½ per cent. The business is not without risk, and matters hardly turned out well in the end for the Isaacs. London itself was ideally suited for the commission houses as it is a large, cosmopolitan European city with a long history as the hub of the world's financial systems. The support services and expertise in international trade, foreign exchange brokerage, financing and communications are all available in one place. Where better to be in the international military supply brokerage business than London? It provided the 19th century equivalent of international one-stop shopping. (6) One self-indulgent fantasy of US Civil War buffs is that all the brokered military equipment from Britain went to America, either North or South. Au contraire, there were wars going on large and small elsewhere through the 1860s in Brazil, New Zealand, Italy, Mexico, and so on. Many foreign governments brought British military supplies during this period in history.

It also assists in understanding that at this point in British history the *Ashkenazi* Jews, of which the Isaacs were descendants, are at best considered second class citizens of London with limited rights. In fact, only from mid-19th century onward were they even considered 'citizens' at all, before then they were tolerated inhabitants. (7) As Isaac D'Israeli noted in 1797, "This British land which when the slave touches he becomes free, retains the child of Jacob in abject degradation. He cannot own the house in which he inhabits, and is not able to elevate himself among his horde by professions which might ennoble his genius and dignify his people." The widespread opposing point of view was more or less echoed throughout Europe at the time, and was summarized as follows: The Jews are a very distant class of the inhabitants of London consisting of perhaps 20,000…though a few of them are respectable characters, the majority are notorious "sharpers". (8) Dishonest or not, the British Jews were allowed to do business as brokers and many were successful in that line of work. *Shepardim* Jews of Middle Eastern descent were quicker to abandon Judaism with the repeal of the few rights contained in the 'Jew Bill' (1753), and either converted to the Church of England or practiced no religion at all. However, the *Ashkenazim* remained rabbinic, stayed in their insular communities and supported their synagogues in a more traditional way. Jewish emancipation in Britain dates from the passage of another bill in 1845 that permitted most rights of citizenship, except for election to Parliament. In contrast, the Confederacy was very open to Jews, and several high ranking officers and members of the Jefferson Davis cabinet were Jews. This would never have happened in the North. (9) The Isaacs had a large network of suppliers, including their own shoe factory, leased by Turner Bros, Hyde & Co, which supplied leatherwork and shoes from Northampton (entirely for export). Another of the firm's suppliers was Smith, Kemp & Wright of Birmingham, who produced buttons with the SIC & Co back-mark. Other firms which supplied military goods brokered by SIC & Co included the following:

JE Barnett & Co (Enfield rifles) London
Walter H Hindley (Cotton sheeting and bagging) London
Richards & Co (Cotton items) London
Reynolds & Son (Wharfage and warehousing) London
R & W Aston (Enfield Rifles) Birmingham
Fortnum & Mason (Food stuffs for blockade runners) London
Savory & Moore (Medicines) London
John Hall & Sons (Muskets and gunpowder) London
Davenport & Co (Earthenware and china)
Robinson & Fleming (Gunpowder)
William Essex & Sons (Curriers)
John Churchill (Medical books) London (10)

S. Isaac, Campbell & Co also opened a branch in Nassau, on New Providence Island in the Bahamas, just to administer the tremendous quantity of goods shipped from England, and destined for the Confederacy. (11) Eldest son Henry Isaac and Benjamin Woolley Hart superintended the Nassau branch of SIC & Co. Benjamin Hart, Samuel Isaac's brother-in-law, had been living in New York City since 1856. The evidence for Benjamin W. Hart living for a period of time in New York comes from the Louis Heyliger letter to CS Secretary of War Randolph on July 19, 1862 where he wrote:

"Mr Hart is a resident of New York and came out here (Nassau) to superintend the business transactions of the (SIC & Co) London firm." (12)

This is believed to be the origin of the myth about the Isaacs coming from New York City during 1861 and purchasing the fictional, non-existent Campbell commission house in London. The only germ of truth here is the Benjamin Hart/New York connection. Who knows how these things get started? On July 29, 1862, came a terrible personal setback for the Isaacs, the tragic news of the death of 26 year old Henry Isaac from malaria while acting as an agent for SIC & Co in Nassau. Following Henry's untimely departure, Benjamin

W. Hart took full responsibility in accounting for, and warehousing supplies brought in from England, and also dealt with financial correspondence between the islands and the Confederate Government in Richmond.

NOTES:

1. Hoole, William S. *Confederate Foreign Agent: The Civil War Diary of Major Edward C. Anderson, CS,* University of Alabama Publishing, 1976.
2. *The McRae Papers*, South Carolina Confederate Museum and Relic Room. These 10,000 muskets of the old pattern were possibly the P-1851 Minie rifle or the 1842 smoothbore, and between September 25th and October 1st 1861, 700 second hand rifles Pattern of 1851 were inspected, accepted and marked by Isaac Curtis (IC), a viewer working for the firm of S. Isaac, Campbell & Co.
3. Ibid, Hoole
4. United States Government Printing Office, *The War of Rebellion: A compilation of the records of the Union and Confederate Armies*, (1904) Series IV, Volume I, p. 1007-1008
5. Ibid, OR Series IV Volume II, p. 227
6. There were other London commission houses such as Sinclair, Hamilton & Co, that specialized in brokering military supplies. However, SIC & Co worked exclusively with the Confederate Government, whereas others were not as keen to do so, and vice-versa.
7. The *Ashkenazim* were the Jews of European, specifically Germanic descent, which were systematically run out of one country after another during the Middle Ages. The Middle Eastern Jews were known as *Shepardic*.
8. Katz, David, *The Jews in the History of England 1485-1850,* Oxford University Press, 1994, p. 221. The Isaacs (sadly) fit to a tee the horrid, stereotyped description of Jews which was contained in the anonymous book from 1780, *A peep into the Synagogue or a letter to the Jews*.
9. Quartermaster General Abraham Myers, and Attorney General Judah Benjamin to name two prominent examples. As far as the tolerance for Jews in the North, see General U.S. Grant's infamous 'General Order # 11.' See also: Rosen, Robert, *Jews in the Confederacy*, University of South Carolina Press (2000), 544 pages.
10. Ibid, McRae Papers
11. The Bahamas were (and still are) a part of the British Commonwealth

of Nations. Located just off the American coast, the islands served as a base for Confederate blockade runners as well as Rum runners during the 'Noble Experiment' period of American Prohibition (1919-33).

12. Ibid, OR Series IV Volume II, p. 8

RUNNING THE BLOCKADE

The first major shipment of arms and equipment bought by Huse through S. Isaac, Campbell & Co was taken onboard the steamer *Fingal*, which left Greenock, Scotland, on October 10th, 1861. The *Fingal* was purchased in September 1861, for £17,500, and extreme measures were taken to conceal the ship's mission from ever watchful Union agents. She was registered in the name of a British citizen, and arrangements were made to load her by a chartered steamer, so keeping Confederate supplies off the closely watched railways. A mock sale was then arranged by Bulloch's assistant John Low who then travelled across the country to avoid Federal agents. On October 24th, 1861, U.S Secretary of the Navy, Gideon Welles wrote the following to Flag officer Goldsborough, U.S Navy Commander of the blockading Squadron, the following:

"Authentic information has been received that a large quantity of rifles, powder, swords, and munitions of various kinds were shipped near London on board the steamer Colletis, which left the Thames on the 29th ultimo for Greenock, Scotland, when her cargo was to be transferred to the new iron-screw steamer Fingal. The transhipment is made to throw this Government off its guard. The Fingal *is schooner rigged, with two masts, has a round stern, the bust of a man for a head, has one deck and a poop, is 186 feet long and 25 feet wide, and 12 9/10 feet depth of hold. She is British built, and her tonnage is a little short of 500 tons. Her cargo consists of 31,000 pounds powder, 525,000 cartridges, 1,550,000 percussion caps, 1,500 rifled "Brown Bessies" 300 sword bayonets, a large quantity of paper for cartridges, and other articles much needed in the states of insurrection. A contract has also been made in England for a larger amount of similar articles to be shipped by another vessel, which was to follow within two weeks of the* Fingal.*"* (1)

The *Fingal* was actually loaded with some 11,000 Enfield rifles, 500,000 cartridges, over 1,000,000 percussion caps, 3,000 cavalry sabres, 500 revolvers, 2 Blakely cannon, 8,000 shells, 400 barrels of gunpowder, 9,982 yards of blankets, drugs, plus 2,000 rifles for the States of Georgia and Louisiana. Added to this were accoutrements furnished by S. Isaac, Campbell & Co, and over £10,000 worth of accoutrements and leather from A Ross & Co. Also onboard was Major EC Anderson, having completed his mission. She successfully arrived in Savannah on November 14, 1861. (2) As mentioned in the previous letter, another shipment had been contracted for, this shipment of arms and munitions was placed aboard the steamer *Gladiator.*

On November 9, 1861 J.B. Marchand Commander of the U.S.S James Adger, wrote to Welles from Southampton, England:

" Information has been given me that an iron propeller named Gladiator, of London, of 600 tons burden, left the Thames two days ago laden with 600 cases of Enfield and Belgian rifles, a number of cannon, a large quantity of field blankets, shells, powder, and other munitions of war, bound either to Bermuda or Nassau, the latter the most probable, with the intention of transhipment to the Southern States. The Gladiator is an English vessel with regular papers and destined to an English port". (3)

The *Gladiator* also carried: mess tins, blankets, medicine, gunpowder, cartridges, surgical equipment, and percussion caps supplied by SIC & Co.

Another ship with a huge amount of stores purchased by Huse through SIC & Co was the *Economist;* surviving invoices from the McRae Papers confirm this. Invoices dated 16th December, 1861 for *"Oxford Grey Army Cloth"* and another dated December 14, 1861 for *"Blue Grey Army Cloth"* plus others dated December 23, and December 31, 1861, this time for accoutrements, attest to this. (4) On February 14, 1861, the United States Minister in Brussels, Belgium, wrote: *"The cargo of the Economist is looked upon as one of the most important yet dispatched".* (5) Backing up this dispatch was a letter from the U.S Consulate in London, F.H Morse, who wrote on March 14th 1861:

"Economist and Southwick have near 40,000 Enfield rifles, with a large

quantity of powder, rifled cannon, army clothing, etc on board for the Insurgent States". (6)

As well the *Economist and Fingal,* S. Isaac, Campbell & Co would go on to charter the steamers *Southwick, Gladiator, Sea Queen, Sir William Peel, Springbok, and Stephen Hart and Harriet Pinckney* to ship their Confederate orders. Three of these vessels, the *Southwick, Stephen Hart and Harriet Pinckney,* were certainly owned by SIC & Co. Proof that two of them were property of the firm comes in a letter written by Charles Kuhn Prioleau of Fraser, Trenholm & Co to Captain J.H. North written on February 6, 1862, which stated:

"I have received your private letter of the 5th instant and that of your firm, the latter formally turning over to me the vessel lately built by Messrs Fawcett, Preston & Co. In reply to your request that I should take charge of the ship referred to I have to say that I accept the vessel and request that you will cause a crew to be shipped for her, capable of navigating her across the Atlantic, and that you will have the ship sent to the port of London. This is to be done in case she can be put under English colors and her name to be changed to the Harriet Pinckney. *In taking out the register for the ship, her owners may be given as S. Isaac, Campbell & Co, who are prepared to sign such papers as may be necessary to make the transfer legal. SIC & Co, as you are aware, are the owners of the S (Southwick) and they are willing to charter or purchase the* Harriet Pinckney." *(7)*

On January 29, 1862, the Stephen Hart was captured by the Union vessel Supply off the Florida coast carrying a full cargo of accoutrements, cloth, and armaments. The proof that she was loaded with army supplies for the Confederacy was so complete the Isaacs' attorney did not defend the rights of the owners. On March 19, 1862 her cargo was examined by an appraiser, Orison Blunt. (8) The cargo consisted of large quantities of small arms, ordnance supplies, accoutrements, cloth, and shoes. Among the captured cargo was listed: 1,546 yards of gray army cloth, 11,543 yards of steel mixed gray cloth for uniforms, 625 gross CSA buttons, 2,220 water proof covers for mess tins, plus a huge quantity of buttons for army uniforms and clothing, including black wooden buttons, bone buttons, and horn buttons. It was after this incident with the Stephen Hart that all army supplies were carried by ship to Nassau or Bermuda only, and from there run through the blockade in fast shallow drafted ships.

In late 1862 came one of the largest shipments of war materiel supplied by S. Isaac, Campbell & Co to take place during the entire war. This shipment was made by the steamer *Justitia*, and arrived safely in December 1862.
The original SIC & Co invoice spanned thirty six pages, and covered goods including:

Surgical instruments, telegraph wire, brandy and, intriguingly, even twenty sets of scales.
Items for the Quartermaster Department included:
Blankets, cloth, facing cloth, greatcoats, buttons, and also vast amounts of leather, which included:
30 Waxed backs for ball bags,
300 Pouch middlings
300 Belt middlings
250 Waist belt middlings
500 Knapsack sling middlings
642 lbs cut leather for knapsack trimmings,
150 Middlings for gun slings. (9)

By mid-1862, S. Isaac, Campbell & Co attempted to enter into discussions with the Confederate Government in Richmond for the supply of vast amounts of clothing and equipment to Confederate troops. In a letter dated November 17, 1862, Benjamin W Hart, the SIC & Co agent in Nassau, wrote to George W Randolph, CS Secretary of War:

" My friends Messrs S. Isaac, Campbell & Co, of London, instructed me to address your proposals to furnish clothing and equipment for 100,000 men, deliverable at Bermuda or Nassau, which have failed to reach you owing to the capture of the vessel by which they were forwarded. I now take the opportunity to repeat the proposals to the following effect;
Messrs S. Isaac, Campbell & Co request me to state that there exists now greater facilities for procuring the materials required by the Confederate Government than prevailed in the early part of the war, when they were scarce and difficult to procure. Under these circumstances they feel confident of their ability to give satisfaction to the Department in respect to the quality of the equipments and the dispatch which they can be completed, which they would be able to accomplish in about three months from receipt of order". (10)

John B Jones, a clerk working in the War Department in Richmond noted in his diary on December 24th, 1862 that "...*A Mr Hart, agent for S Isaac Campbell & Co London, proposes to clothe and equip 100,000 men for us, and to receive certificates for specific amounts of cotton. This same house has, it is said, advanced as much as $ 2,000,000 on our account. This looks cheering. We have credit abroad." (11)*

Back in Richmond, a sceptical Quartermaster General A.C. Myers wrote on December 30th 1862:

" Respectfully returned to the Secretary of War.
I have considered this communication, and submit that it contains nothing upon which to base a report. The proposal is to clothe 100,000 men, but no item of cost of the clothing is presented. Major JB Ferguson, of the Quartermaster's Department, is now in Europe for the purpose of making purchases for the Department. The parties can make their proposals directly to him, and he can best determine upon the expediency of accepting the proposition of these parties." (12)

The *Stephen Hart* however, turned out not to be the only ship lost, for on February 3rd, 1863 whilst making for the harbour of Nassau, the *Springbok* was captured by the Union gunboat *Sonoma*. The cargo that was captured was significant, and included the following items:

220 bags of coffee, 300 chests of tea, 4 cases of ginger, 19 bags pimento, 10 bags of cloves, 60 bags of pepper, 53 packages of medicines and saltpetre, 18 bales of army blankets, butternut color, seven bales of army cloth. 20 bales gray cloth, 4 bales men's colored travelling shirts, 540 pairs Gray Army Blankets, and 24 pairs white blankets, 360 gross brass navy buttons, marked CSN, 10 gross army buttons marked "C" 397 gross buttons marked "I", and 148 gross buttons marked "A", 555 gross in total, all buttons marked on underside "S. Isaac, Campbell & Co / 71 Jermyn St London". The finds went on: *8 cavalry sabres, 11 sword bayonets, 992 pairs of army boots, 97 pairs of russet brogans, and finally 47 pairs of cavalry boots.* (13)

The enigmatic letter of instruction to the master on board was thus:

"LONDON December 8th 1862
CAPTAIN JAMES MAY
Dear Sir- your vessel being now loaded, you will proceed at once to the port of Nassau, NP, and on arrival report yourself to Mr BW Hart there, who will give you orders as to the delivery of your cargo and any further information you require.
We are, dear sir & c SPEYER & HEYWOOD"

The letter to the agent of the consignee directed BW Hart, Nassau and from these same persons, Speyer & Heywood, was thus:

"Under instructions from Messrs Isaac, Campbell & Co, of Jermyn St, we enclose the bills of lading for goods shipped on the "Springbok" consigned to you." (14)

What caused one blockade runner to be caught while another made multiple voyages without ever seeing a Union warship? The laws of probability certainly played a role, as did the craftiness of the ship captain. Under the command of Lt. John Wilkinson, the famous Confederate owned blockade runner *Robert E. Lee* made twenty one successful runs through the Union blockade. One of his tricks was to fly the stars and stripes once out in open sea. He once exchanged salutes with the captain of a Union gunboat passing by closely. How it could have been mistaken for a commercial US vessel is hard to comprehend.

The *Robert E. Lee* was painted to blend in with the ocean, smoke stacks were angled back and the engines burned anthracite (which produced less smoke), unless a smoke screen was to their advantage. Wilkinson once had his engine crew shovel in coal dust to create a thick cloud of smoke around dusk; while the Union ship chasing him steered toward the smoke, he altered course and slipped away into the night. They only attempted the harbour on moonless nights under the cover of darkness. One sailor complained to the ship captain about the danger of running at night without lights, and voiced his concern about colliding with another ship. The captain replied, Perhaps…but if we run our lights we will collide with a cannon ball. (15) They proceeded without lights with a good lookout posted. The *Robert E. Lee* was so notorious that on each trip they had to pass through 20 to 30 Federal warships and the task was not made easier when the cargo was gunpowder and ammunition.

How profitable were the blockade runners? A good example of the lucrative (though potentially short lived) nature of the blockade running trade was the ship *Banshee*, a British owned vessel which operated out of Nassau and Bermuda. She was captured on her seventh run into Wilmington, North Carolina, and confiscated by the U.S. Navy for use as a blockading warship. However, at the time of her capture, she had already turned a 700% profit for her owners, who quickly commissioned and built the *Banshee No. 2*, which soon joined the firm's fleet of blockade runners. One well known "toast" went as follows: ***"Here's to the Southern planters who grow the cotton; to the Yankees that maintain the blockade and keep the prices of cotton up; and to the Limeys who buy the cotton. So, three cheers for a long continuance of the war, and success to the blockade runners!"*** (16)

It was believed that with as little as two successful runs through the Union blockade, a ship had already made a profit for its owners. With the bookkeeping methods of the Isaacs, their odds of profit were much better than that. One source opined that if the Isaacs lost two out of three shipments to the Union blockade, they would still make an overall profit on the one that got through. (17)

Photo # NH 63888   Blockade runner Robert E. Lee, later USS Fort Donelson. Artwork by Erik Heyl

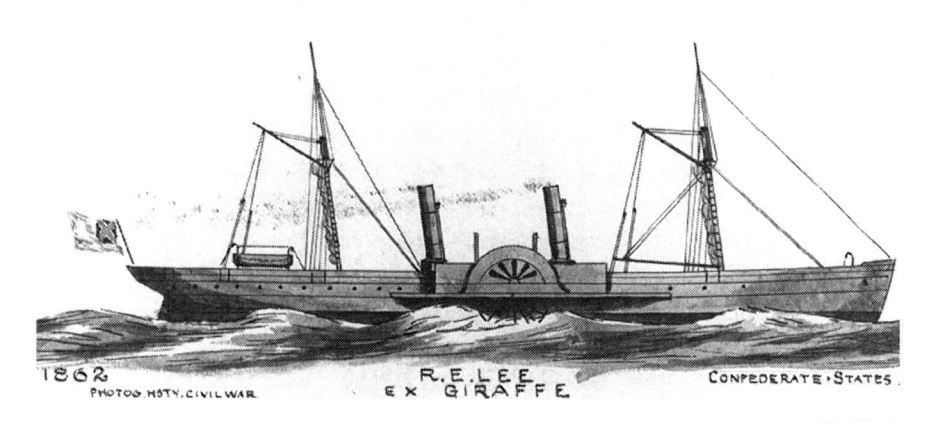

The R.E. LEE
Watercolour by Erik Heyl 1951. (Courtesy Naval Historical Center)

53

NOTES:

1. Official Records of the Union and Confederate Navies in the War of the Rebellion *Series I Volume 6 p 355-356.* An original SIC & Co invoice from the McRae Papers shows that 6,210 army blankets were to sail on the *Fingal.*
2. Wise, Stephen R: *Lifeline of the Confederacy: Blockade Running during the Civil War,* University of South Carolina Press, 1988, p. 53.
3. Official Records of the Union and Confederate Navies in the War of the Rebellion, US Government Printing Office, Washington, DC (1904) *Series 1 Volume 1 p 202*
4. The McRae Papers
5. Ibid, OR. *Series 1 Volume 7, p. 107*
6. Ibid, OR *Series 1 Volume 7, p. 218.*
7. Ibid, OR *Series1 Volume 2 p. 143.* Note: Charles Kuhn Prioleau, was a native of Charleston S.C. he was manager and partner in the firm Fraser, Trenholm & Co of 10 Rumford Place, Liverpool. He was heavily involved in the purchase of vessels and ancillary goods for the Confederacy. The *Stephen Hart* was named after Samuel Isaac's father in law, (Samuel was married to Emma Hart). Harriet Pinckney was the maiden name of Mrs. Caleb Huse, hence it is reasonably clear that the blockade runner *Harriet Pinckney* was named after her.
8. Orison Blunt was an appraiser appointed by the prize court. He was a crony of Abraham Lincoln from New York... and one of his few supporters in that city. Blunt had a small Ordnance Department contract to provide US-made P53s. Very few arms were ever produced and his contract was cancelled when the barrels failed proof. The famous Claud E. Fuller gun collection at Chickamauga/Chattanooga (CHCH) National Battlefield Park has a well-preserved example of a Blunt contract Enfield on display.
9. The McRae Papers. *Middling* is a term for leather that is neither good nor bad. It is where the saying *Fair to middling* comes from.
10. Official Records of the Union and Confederate Navies. *Series 2 Volume 2 p. 605*
11. Jones, John B. *A Rebel War Clerks Diary.* Sagamore Press 1958.
12. OR Series IV Volume II p191.
13. U.S. Supreme Court. *The Springbok*, 72 U.S. 5 Wall. 1 1 (1866) **Note: A huge amount of "russet brogans" are accounted for in the existing SIC & Co invoices in the McRae papers.**
14. Ibid *See Appendix*

15. Underwood, Rodman L. *Waters of Discord*, McFarland Publishing Co, 2003, p. 58.
16. Earp, Charles Albert, *Father John B.Tabb Aboard Confederate Blockade Runners*, America's Civil War, published by Weider History Group, January 1996.
17. Wilson, Harold, *Confederate Industry: Manufacturers and Quartermasters in the Civil War,* University of Mississippi Press, 2002, p. 161. 97 96

THE ERLANGER LOAN

On November 1st, 1862 Benjamin Woolley Hart, the S. Isaac, Campbell & Co agent based in Nassau, wrote to Colonel Josiah Gorgas enclosing the following invoice for unpaid stores: This statement was enclosed in a letter by Gorgas to Secretary of War Seddon on December 26th, 1862.

Abstract of statement showing amount due to S. Isaac, Campbell & Co, contractors for C.S. Ordnance stores, dated November 1st, 1862, forwarded by Benjamin W Hart, Agent of S. Isaac, Campbell & Co, Nassau;

August 23, 1862 balance, £45,038
July 15, 1862- Steamship Columbia, £44,500
August 27, 1862, - Steamship Harriet Pinckney, £120,162.7
August 27, 1862, - Ouachita, £8,000
Oct 1 1862, - Rifles, etc, Vienna, £175,000
Oct 1 1862,- Scabbards, etc, £12,000
Oct 30 1862, - Justitia shipment, - £120,000
Nov1 1862, - Steamship Cornubia, - £24,000
Nov 1 1862, - Steamship Justitia, - £20,000
Nov 1 1862, - Cornubia Shipment, - £8,000
Interest - £6,000

TOTAL £582,700.7   (1)

By January 13th 1863, Hart was forced to write to Confederate Secretary of State Judah P Benjamin the following letter:

"I am instructed by our London house most respectfully but most earnestly to pray your attention to our account for military supplies furnished to your

government, which has now reached the amount of half a million sterling and will soon extend to £600,000, when orders now in hand for ordnance are executed. We feel assured that you will so well understand the urgent necessities for money pressing upon our house under such circumstances that so far from needing any apology for asking large remittances on account of it at the very earliest moment you will most cordially concur in acknowledging our claims to the attentive and prompt consideration of the cabinet and the Government.

Since the very incipiency of the struggle in which the Confederate States have been and continue to be engaged we have afforded them every assistance in our power, and we refer with unmixed satisfaction to the testimonials and kind acknowledgements from yourself when administering the War Department of the services we have rendered to the State in the infancy of the war, when our resources in money and credit were placed without limit at its disposal and probably contributed in some degree to the success of its armies in the field.

We sincerely and earnestly trust that the claims of our house are not forgotten or if temporarily in oblivion will be revived by our present and earnest appeal to the attention of the Government. During the months that have passed since the date of your letter the indebtedness of the Government to us has been largely increasing and we have continued to furnish supplies and to hope on from month to month that the remittances which we were promised to us would arrive.

In conclusion, we again most earnestly crave your attention and that of the cabinet and Government to our solicitations, at the same time embracing the opportunity to assure you that we are desirous of continuing to place our services and our resources at the disposal of the Government of the Confederate States".

In a further letter written on the same day also to Benjamin, Hart went on to further stress the importance of prompt payment by the Confederate Government:

"Referring to our previous letter of this date, we feel ourselves impelled still further to represent to you the extreme urgencies of our house for money and the critical condition in which we are placed from the absence of the remittances we have so long and so anxiously looked forward to, and it is not without great pain we apprise you that we find ourselves much

embarrassed, which may be increased to the most serious point unless we receive the most immediate relief from the Government.

We venture further, most respectfully, to represent to you that a crisis in the affairs of our house would, in our humble opinion as mercantile men, exercise a most pernicious and withering influence on the credit of the Confederate Government in foreign countries for the abandonment of friends whom you have so kindly mentioned as 'having exhibited toward the Government a kind and generous confidence at a moment when all others in foreign countries seem to be doubtful, timorous and wavering' could do no otherwise than produce an impression not easily to be effaced from the sensitive minds of commercial and moneyed men.

We venture also to hope that our representations may receive the attentions of the cabinet, and that immediate relief may be dispatched to us. Our immediate wants are £120,000, and we trust to receive a considerable portion of this by return of steamer, the balance of our account in the succeeding month at furthest, and at least the same amount in the same periods ensuing. The receipt of these funds will enable us to proceed with our business with advantage and place us in a position to enable us to continue to furnish the Government with military supplies." (2)

The Confederacy had cotton, and needed money. Their strategy of King Cotton, which involved taking their best and most reliable form of raising capital and sitting on it, had been a dismal failure. Hence, the Confederate Government offered bonds backed by Treasury Department controlled cotton supplies as collateral for what amounted to a line of credit. Rumours of the arrangement had been circulating around Europe in early 1863 and made their way back to the United States through diplomatic channels. The United States minister to France wrote in a letter dated February 13, 1863 to Secretary of State William H. Seward, *"A correspondent of the London Post says he learned that a Confederate loan for five millions £ sterling has been negotiated through the house of Erlanger and Co. in conjunction with the leading capitalists of London and Liver-pool...the truth of this statement is at least doubtful. Your means of judging it are as good or better than my own."* (3) A month later on March 13, 1863 he wrote again to Seward on the matter, but by this time he was more informed and *"... inclined to believe that arrangements have been made with the House of Erlanger & Co. Frankfurt, to loan the Confederates three millions £."* (4)

Who was Erlanger & Co? According to the US minister to France, this House of Erlanger is a *German Jew house* having its principal place of business in Frankfurt with branches or agencies at other points, one of which is here (Paris). (5) Erlanger was quite a bit more than that, and his bank was more than a *Jew house*, whatever that means. Baron Emile Erlanger was one of the wealthiest men in Europe, and this German (and Jewish) banker had branches in Amsterdam, as well as Paris and Frankfurt. The bonds came to Erlanger in December 1862 after the Confederacy failed to find a British bank to float them. (6) After several weeks of negotiations with Erlanger and Co, the financier sent three agents to Richmond to propose a much larger bond issuance, as cotton was then selling for sixty to eighty cents per pound, and the bonds were redeemable for cotton at the rate of ten cents per pound. The Confederates demurred, and the Erlanger or cotton loan as it became known was able to raise the not insignificant sum of $15,000,000 (CS) or £3 million for the Confederate Government to purchase much needed war materiel from Europe. However, it could have easily been two or three times that amount. These bonds were denominated in £ Sterling and French Francs, and offered in the European cities of Amsterdam, Frankfurt, Liverpool, London, and Paris, the exchange rate was to be $5.00 (Confederate) = £1 Sterling. These were actually very favourable terms as in 1860 the exchange rate was $4.86 (US) = £1 Sterling. (7) Their terms would never be that generous again. There are still historians who speculate that if the Confederates had followed Erlanger's advice on leveraging the cotton bonds in January 1863, the Confederacy would have had a permanent history. (8)

The bonds sold at 90% face value, and were redeemable for Confederate Government owned cotton in the Confederacy itself. This last clause had a critical effect in stimulating blockade running, because the holders of Erlanger bonds had to risk the Federal blockade to convert the bonds into cotton. The subscription opened on March 19, 1863, initially these cotton bonds were very successful, with the most prominent and wealthy people in England making investments. The full list of British subscribers was as follows:
Sir Henry de Houghton, Bart £180,000

Isaac, Campbell & Co, of 71 Jermyn St London, army contractors £150,000
Thomas Stirling Begbie 50 Mansion House Place, London, Ship owner £140,000

The Marquis of Bath £50,000
James Spence, Liverpool, correspondent of the Times £50,000
Mr Beresford Hope £40,000
George Edward Seymour, stock broker, Throgmorton St London £40,000
Messrs Fernie £30,000
Alex Collie & partners £20,000
Fleetwood, Patten, Wilson, L Schuster, directors of Union Bank, London £20,000
W. S. Lindsay £20,000
Sir Coutts Lindsay, Baronet £20,000
John Laird, MP, Birkenhead £20,000
M B Sampson City Editor Times £15,000
John Thaddeuus Delane, Editor Times £10,000
Lady Georgina Fane (Sister of Lord Westmoreland) £15,000
JS Gilliat, Director Bank of England £10,000
D Forbes Campbell 45 Dover St, Piccadilly London £30,000
George Peacock, MP £5,000
Lord Wharncliffe £5,000
WH Gregory MP £4,000
WJ Rideout, proprietor London Morning Post £4,000
Edward Akenroyd £1,500
Lord Campbell £1,000
Lord Donoughomore £1,000
Lord Richard Grosvenor £1,000
Hon Evelyn Ashley, son of Lord Shaftesbury, and private secretary to Lord Palmerston £500
Right Hon, William Ewart Gladstone £2,000.

This adds up to grand total of £1,214,500. (9) The subscription sales might not have been so robust but for an incorrect assumption on the part of British investors. As the US Consol in Liverpool reported back to Secretary of State William Henry Seward, "...*as strange as it may seem, these people here who are aiding the Rebels and taken or purchased these bonds believe if worse comes, and the Union is restored, the United States Government will assume payment of their bonds.*" (10) He was surprised at that, but allowed that the Erlanger loan had an immediate and positive effect on the Confederate purchasing operations. In fairness to the investors who badly miscalculated the munificence of Uncle Sam, the Confederate loans were still backed by $45 million worth of cotton, grossly over-collateralized as Erlanger had previously pointed out. On May 25, 1863, Emile Erlanger, Jr. on behalf of Erlanger & Co made an agreement with S. Isaac, Campbell & Co to take over the company's account and recover the sum of £515,000 owed them by the Confederate Government.

As part of the agreement for Erlanger taking over the account, Caleb Huse was to give a certificate of indebtedness to SIC & Co, in return Erlanger was to give SIC & Co £150,000 of Erlanger (Cotton Loan) bonds for which they had already subscribed. S. Isaac, Campbell & Co was to have another £150,000 worth of the Erlanger bonds, plus £90,000, which Erlanger & Co advanced SIC &Co.

SIC & Co, in turn, was to leave in the hands of Erlanger & Co the cotton warrants and 8 per cent bonds now deposited with latter for the security of their advance of £90,000. SIC & Co was to have a full £300,000 worth of Erlanger bonds, half of these to be delivered no later than June 15, 1863. It was agreed that SIC & Co remain responsible to the Confederate Government for their account, and that SIC & Co was to have their account audited by Colin McRae. (11)

Huse wrote to Erlanger & Co the following day, May 26, 1863 the following:
"Gentlemen:
S Isaac Campbell & Co have an account with the Confederate States Government for army supplies furnished by them on my order, upon which account there is due a balance of, say, £515,000. This amount I agree on the part of the Confederate States Government may be transferred to yourselves upon any terms that may be agreed upon between yourselves and Isaac, Campbell & Co, and I further agree that, provided the account is thus transferred to you, all the money that I may receive from any source for the payment of this claim shall be paid to you." (12)

Caleb Huse then wrote to McRae on June 12, 1863 stating:
"As security for the payment of their account I have deposited with them cotton warrants representing £100,000 and 8 per cent bonds for $2,000,000. Upon these securities Messrs Erlanger & Co have advanced to S. Isaac, Campbell & Co the sum of £90,000. Messrs Erlanger & Co have further arranged with S. Isaac, Campbell & Co to take over their entire account." (13)

NOTES:

1. Letters received by the Confederate Secretary of War, Record Group 109, US National Archives.
2. Official Records of the Union and Confederate Navies in the War of the Rebellion, Series II Volume II p641- 643.
3 Seward, William H. *Papers Relating to Foreign Affairs: Diplomatic Correspondence*, US Government Printing Office, 1864, Volume I, p. 643. Letter from Union minister to France, William Dayton dated February 13, 1863.
4. The Civil War: Diaries and Collected Papers: *William Lewis Dayton Papers Index, MTSU Library, Murfreesboro, Tennessee. Letter dated March 13, 1863 from Dayton to Seward.*
5. Ibid, *Dayton Papers. Note:* How best to explain the attitude expressed by Dayton to Secretaryy of State Seward? In a word, anti-Semitic, this was prevalent in the North and limited opportunities there. See General US Grant's General Order # 11 expelling the Jews from Union occupied territory. The Confederacy was much more accepting of Jews and Jewish culture. See also: Rosen, Robert M. *Southern Jews in the Civil War*, University of South Carolina Press, (2001) 560 pgs.
6. Lonn, Ella, Foreigners in the Confederacy, UNC Press, 1940, p. 367.
7. Bigelow, John, *"Lest we Forget", Gladstone, Morley and the Confederate loan of 1863,* Published DeVinne Press, London, 1905. Bigelow succeeded Dayton in Paris after he passed away in 1864.
8. See *If We Had the Money* Southern Historical Society Papers, Volume XXXV, p. 201-203.
9. US Government Printing Office: *Official Records of the War of Rebellion for the Union and Confederate Armies*, Series IV volume II p. 888
10. US Consol to Liverpool Thomas Dudley to Secretary of State W.H. Seward, March 23, 1863.
11. Wise, Stephen R., *Lifeline of the Confederacy,* University of South Carolina Press, 1991, p. 94.
12. Ibid, OR
13. Ibid OR p. 645

AGENTS PROVOCATEURS: CRENSHAW AND FERGUSON

At the same time Caleb Huse was acting as purchasing agent for Josiah Gorgas' Ordnance Department, Confederate purchasing agents were being dispatched overseas to procure raw materials, and in some cases finished products for the other departments under Secretary of War James A. Seddon. Major J.B. Ferguson, who had been a purchasing agent for the Confederacy early in the war, was sent to England in September 1862 as the official Quartermaster purchasing agent there. (1) He was assigned to take over procurement of Quartermaster material from Major Caleb Huse, the Ordnance agent. These efforts on the part of Ferguson began to yield large quantities of bulk woollen cloth. James Boswell Ferguson, Jr. arrived in England in December 1862, and after basing his operations in Liverpool, he transferred his base to Manchester to be nearer the woollen mills of Lancashire and Yorkshire. He was at that time sixty years old, and was a compatriot of General Robert E Lee. Ferguson had a little in common with the Isaacs in the sense that he was described as a natural bred merchant. He benefited from more than twenty years' experience in the mercantile profession, having his own import and export business, *Ferguson JB, Jr. Bro & Co*. Cloths, Cassimeres and Vestings at 9 Pearl Street, *Richmond*. He also married well, wed to Emma Henry, the granddaughter of the famous American patriot, Patrick Henry.

Ferguson, though now the official purchasing agent for the QM Department, quickly found himself in direct conflict with Huse in his attempts at buying goods for the Department. Ferguson became so frustrated with Huse's attitude and his lack of cooperation, that on April 18, 1863 he wrote to Abraham Myers, Quartermaster General in Richmond complaining of irregularities on Caleb Huse's dealings with SIC & Co. (2) Ferguson wrote:

"In the first interview I had with Major Huse he informed me that his indebtedness to Messrs S. Isaac, Campbell & Co was, in round numbers £500,000 (the true figure by this time was £515,000) and that over £100,000 had been used for the QM Dept. He (Huse) said it was true that upon some of his purchases he had received a commission, but he intended to use a part of the money to pay his travelling expenses, and the balance, amounting to £1,000 to purchase a military library, which he intended to present to the Ordnance Dept. I expressed the opinion that the amount of commission should have been deducted from the face of his invoices in the shape of a discount, and that I would advise him to postpone his donation to the Ordnance Department until his debts were paid and our army shod and clad. After the meeting was over a conversation occurred between an officer of the navy and myself, the sum and substance of which you will find in a copy of his letter enclosed. The next morning I called at Major Huse's office, and he showed me the invoices of the articles sent out by the Justitia. My familiarity with some of the classes of goods mentioned in said invoice led me to believe that extortionate prices had been charged for them.

I requested Major Huse to show me a sample of the 12,000 yards sent out at 7s (Shillings) 6d (Pennies) per yard. I took a sample of it and feel no hesitation in saying that a similar article can be furnished at from 4s 6d to 4s 10d per yard, equal in every respect to the cloth sent out. From the foregoing you will perceive there were three prominent facts for me to consider; firstly the admission of Major Huse that he had received a commission on some of his purchases; second that the senior partner of the house through whom nearly all of his business had been transacted offered to divide a commission with an officer of the navy, and third that exorbitant prices had been charged for such articles as I could identify."
(3)

As mentioned in the last letter Major Ferguson also accused S. Isaac, Campbell & Co of attempting to bribe a CS Naval officer.

James H North, a Lieutenant in the CS Navy had been ordered to Europe in May 1861 by Secretary of the Navy, Stephen Mallory to work with James Dunwoody Bulloch in the purchase of Ironclad vessels for the navy. In a letter dated April 1st, 1863 North wrote to Major Ferguson the following:

"Dear Sir: Your letter of March 30th has just been received. In that letter you ask me to do you the favor to state in writing the substance of a conversation I had with you shortly after your (my) arrival in this country, touching on an offer made me by S. Isaac, of the firm S. Isaac, Campbell & Co., to divide a commission with me on a business transaction for the Government of the Confederate States, and whether or not I regarded that offer as an attempt to induce me to combine with him (S. Isaac) for the purpose of defrauding the Confederate States Government, and whether I rejected the same on that ground. In reply to the foregoing I would say that the subject of the conversation to which your letter refers may be briefly stated as follows:

I did call on S. Isaac of the firm S. Isaac, Campbell & Co, on a matter of business; that Mr Isaac did in the course of conversation make an offer to divide with me a commission of 5 per cent on a business transaction with the Confederate Government, and that I did regard that offer as an attempt to induce me to enter into a transaction to defraud the Confederate Government, and that I did reject the offer." (4)

These bribes were in fact the traditional way business was conducted with purchasing agents on large contracts by most British commission houses of the day. For example, on September 27, 1861 Major Edward Anderson was offered one by Alexander Ross & Co. In closing a deal for purchases for some £10,000 from Ross & Co Anderson wrote:

"Whilst I sat conversing with him, Mr Ross quietly passed over to me a cheque for two hundred and fifty odd pounds, payable to myself individually, as a return commission for my transaction with him... I knew very well that this was the English way of doing business and that the Government permitted its officers to receive these commissions." (5) Anderson accepted the cheque, but credited it by deposit to the Confederate accounts.

Piling on top of the accusations of Major Ferguson was William G Crenshaw, another Confederate purchasing agent who was buying War Department and naval goods.

Until December 1862, Caleb Huse had served as Confederate purchasing agent abroad for a broad variety of military wares for all the bureaus, though technically Huse was an agent of only the Ordnance Department, and working for Josiah Gorgas. However, by the end of 1862 it had become apparent that additional purchasing agents were needed for other bureaus of the War Department. Abraham Myers dispatched Major James Ferguson to serve as the purchasing agent for the Quartermaster/Commissary Department. At about the same time that Ferguson left for England, Secretary of War James Seddon entered into an agreement with William G. Crenshaw of Richmond to establish a line of private blockade runners for the War Department and the CS navy. (6)

Who was William G. Crenshaw and why was there a change of shipping strategy? William G. Crenshaw was joint owner of one of the largest textile mills in Virginia. It was capable of producing both all-wool materials, as well as wool/cotton blends like cassimere and jean cloth very often used for uniforms. The firm also purchased the output of two smaller mills in Virginia and North Carolina, and employed one of the first power looms set up for making military style blankets in Virginia and North Carolina. Crenshaw and his brothers proposed a partnership whereby they would establish a steamship line to carry quartermaster and commissary stores to the Confederacy. The plan Crenshaw had was to have built at least twelve blockade runners of which the Crenshaw brothers would have a quarter interest (7). Crenshaw came to terms with Secretary of War James Seddon to go to England and enter into a partnership with Alexander Collie who had offices in both Manchester and London. Crenshaw departed for England with Seddon's full blessings, though Seddon had not shared this plan with his staff. Seddon for his part was under the misgiving that Crenshaw was going to help Huse expedite his duties. Actually, the so called Crenshaw line was driven by the potential for enormous profits, with half the cargo space onboard the ships taken by the War Department, one fourth for the Navy Department, and the rest of the space allotted to bring in whatever goods Crenshaw and Collie pleased. The Crenshaw/Collie goods brought in would be import duty-free, and the supplies, ships etc they purchased for the government would bring them a 2 ½ percent commission. The pact with Crenshaw was made without the knowledge of Huse or Slidell, who were in France working on the Erlanger loan. (8)

Crenshaw arrived in England in January 1863; once there he quickly came to terms with Collie, and they set up a joint venture for a private steamship line. Major JB Ferguson, a fellow Virginian already in London was in full support of Crenshaw and this venture, and Crenshaw planned to load onboard the

new ships all the goods purchased by Ferguson, as well as the profitable luxury items from which they all stood to profit. All of this was done without the knowledge of the Ordnance Department purchasing agent Caleb Huse, and he was shocked by what he learned. Huse refused to sanction Crenshaw's purchases because he thought it was best to keep all the business in the hands of S. Isaac, Campbell & Co. It was also clear to Huse that Crenshaw was clearly profiteering, and the sizeable cargo space not devoted to military stores was not helping the war effort or the Confederacy.
In explaining this claim, Huse wrote to Crenshaw on April 11, 1863.

"Dear Sir,
Referring to the conversation I had with you on the subject of your mission to Europe, I have to say that in compliance with the instructions of the War Department I will keep you informed of the wants of the War Department as I may from time to time receive them... As regards the purchase of supplies for the Ordnance and Medical Departments, I shall make the purchases without availing myself of the services of Messrs Crenshaw & Collie, excepting in such cases as I may feel satisfied their agency would be advantageous to the Confederate States Government" (9)

Three days later Huse again wrote to Crenshaw.
April 14, 1863

"In the purchase of army supplies....much better can be transacted by the house with which I have had my large transactions, which transactions have received the unqualified approval of the War Department."

Huse also included in the letter the following rebuke to Crenshaw:

"...In communication with you on Saturday last I informed you that I was not prepared to place the purchasing of the Ordnance and medical supplies in your hands...I have not received any instruction from the War Department from which I can draw the influence that I am to do so....The Government has already four steamers the Giraffe, Cornubia, Merrimac, and Eugenie engaged in running the blockade and I have instructions to purchase a fifth. These steamers would have to be idle or be sold if I were to turn over to you the purchasing and forwarding of supplies for the Ordnance and Medical Departments." (10)

Crenshaw was put off by Huse's uncooperative attitude on the matter, and sensing a threat to his profiteering venture, Crenshaw decided to bypass Huse or Gorgas and wrote directly to Secretary of War Seddon on May 5, 1863. His caustic five page letter reads, (in part):

"Since my meeting with Major Huse I have been very much embarrassed by the course I ought to pursue. Every officer here to whom I have had occasion to explain the arrangements I am endeavouring to carry out expresses himself as highly pleased with it except Major Huse. Then naturally I am led to inquire, why does it not meet his views? I have no hesitation in saying that it is because it takes from the hands of Isaac, Campbell & Co the purchase of the Government goods.
This is the true, and, in my opinion, the only reason. Why is he so anxious to retain this business in their hands? He says because they have been so liberal with our Government. I say, no; it is not in their nature to be liberal. They have never had credit here for anything of the sort, and when it is told they have advanced £500,000 for 2 ½ percent commission it bears its own falsity in its own face. They were formally contractors with the English Government, but were dismissed as such, and their contracts cancelled by the Secretary of War in May 1858, for alleged bribery of one of its officers. They remonstrated and tried to explain it was a loan of £500, and not a gift to the receiving officer, but the Secretary of War adhered to his determination and refused to reinstate them.

It is true that they went before a committee appointed to examine into the corruption of the Crimean war generally, and in 1859, on the evidence of one of the firm (S Isaac), the committee reported it was a loan to the officer, although there was no evidence taken of the debt, and was altogether a very loose transaction. As far as I can learn the English Government has since ventured to do but little with them directly.
You have doubtless before you evidence that they offered to bribe one of our own officers last year. You know whether there was anything in Captain North's character to justify them in making to him such a proposition without daring to make the same to others who had been dealing largely with them for more than a year. At all events, the scorn with which Captain North refused it showed that they would have been quite as safe to have made such a proposal to any one else. Major Huse admitted both to Major Ferguson and Captain North that he had received some commission on

government purchases since he had been here, which he intended to apply to the payment of his expenses here and the purchase of a library to send as a present to the Ordnance Bureau, but finding the Government so pressed for money he had paid the amount over to the credit of his account with Isaac, Campbell & Co. Mr White, a commissioner sent here by the State of North Carolina, who has had some opportunity of seeing something of Isaac, Campbell & Co, informs me that he entertains of them the same opinion that I do; nor have I seen any man since my arrival here who would say a good word for them except Major Huse.

Believing it absolutely necessary that all government business here should be under one control, when I heard of the appointment of Major Huse I thought it a move in the right direction, and met him (without prejudice, except that he was from the North) with every desire to co-operate with him.
I am satisfied from what I see and hear that he is not fit for the position, and I sincerely trust it will be your pleasure to select someone now in the Confederate States of high character for integrity and honor, of great business capacity, to come over here and take charge entirely of the financial and commercial affairs of our government. Let the orders of every description come directly to him, and by him executed through that party that he thinks will do it best. He should have entire control of the finances here, with discretionary power to apply the funds (when enough for all purposes are not to be had) to those in his opinion the most important. Of course it is difficult to find such a man, but we have found a man fit to be president of the Confederate States and others to form a cabinet, we can find a man fit to occupy the position.
I suggest, and we can find him, too, among our native born Southerners.
I remain my dear sir, yours ever truly,

WM. G CRENSHAW"(11)

Considering the tone of the letter, and the allegations it contained, both stated and inferred (*he was from the North*), this required some attention. Worse still, it was very similar to the inciting allegations of impropriety recently received from Major Ferguson. While awaiting a reply from Seddon concerning Huse, Crenshaw continued to purchase commissary supplies and ran up a sizeable debt of £115,334 without ever delivering a single cargo. At the end of May, Crenshaw undiplomatically demanded funds from Huse to pay down part of this debt but Huse was resolute and (of course) refused.

On May 18th 1863 Secretary of War James A Seddon wrote to Colonel Josiah Gorgas, Chief of Ordnance and Huse's superior, the following note:
"This matter appears of serious nature. The taking of a commission is altogether inconsistent with the purpose and duty of a trusted agent of the Department. The matter should be fully investigated". (12)

James A. Seddon C.S.A.

By June 1863, Confederate purchasing operations in England were seriously affected. To produce an immediate truce and get back on track, Seddon limited Caleb Huse to Ordnance and medical supply procurement, and Crenshaw was given control over all commissary and quartermaster goods.

Caleb Huse, gravely concerned by the allegations, wrote to McRae on October 20th, 1863:

"I have not only been personally annoyed by the conduct of Major Ferguson and Mr Crenshaw, but my efficiency as an agent for the CS War Department has been seriously impaired to such an extent that I think it is important that my character for integrity and soundness of judgement should be fully re-established; or failing this, that some other officer should be detailed for the important duty to which I have been assigned." (13)

Josiah Gorgas was totally aghast of the charges levelled against Huse and immediately sprang to his defence, knowing he was a capable and loyal officer and suspecting that Crenshaw was in this for profit only. Huse had earned Gorgas' respect with his purchases of both Quartermaster and Ordnance supplies to this time, and to this end Gorgas wrote to Seddon of his suspicions concerning the allegations, writing on May 22nd, 1863:

"Major Huse is an officer of nearly fifteen years service. He knows perfectly well that the naked transaction of taking a commission on purchase, on receiving, directly or indirectly, compensation for purchases for the government, would dismiss him from the service with disgrace; yet he makes confession of this flagrant crime to a stranger in his very first interview with him. It is unnecessary to suggest the propriety of at least hearing Major H.'s statement."

Gorgas continued:

"The matter of Major Huse's unfitness for making purchases is assumed by the Quartermaster- General probably on the testimony of Major Ferguson. I think it proper to say that I am perfectly satisfied with his business capacities, and so far as that is concerned desire no change". (14)

Colin J. McRae, the Confederacy's chief financial agent for Europe who was in England to oversee the Erlanger loan, was appointed to examine the accounts and vouchers of Caleb Huse with particular attention to the financial transactions with SIC & Co. (15)

Crenshaw and Ferguson were not the last to interfere with Confederate Government operated blockade runners. Secretary of War Seddon unwisely failed to grasp the obvious conflict of interest with businessmen and profiteers in the mix with CS purchasing agents or the potential all this had for interdepartmental rivalries of the sort demonstrated here. Seddon continued to ship with privately owned blockade runners, as well as the three or four government owned vessels. And as a result, the Confederacy would struggle to meet all of its needs.

NOTES:

1. Jensen, Leslie D., *Confederate Issue Jackets Part One*, Journal of the Company of Military Historians, Volume 41, # 3 (Fall 1989).
2. United States War Department, *Official Records of the Union and Confederate Armies in the War of Rebellion*, series IV Volume II p.555-556.
3. Ibid p. 558, *An appropriation for $2,000,000 was made at the second session of Congress, per act # 117, approved May 10, 1861, to purchase and construct in France or England, one or more ironclad vessels-of-war for the CS Navy, and Lt J H North, an officer of high standing in the service, was at once sent abroad to procure them if possible.*
4. Ibid, OR Series IV Volume II p558
5. Hoole, W.S. *Confederate Foreign Agent: The European Diary of Major Edward C Anderson,* Confederate Publishing Company, 1976, p. 63
6. Wise, Stephen, *Lifeline of the Confederacy*, University of South Carolina Press, 1991, p. 101.
7. Actually it was spilt as 1/8 share to Crenshaw and 1/8 share to Collie.
8. Ibid, Wise, p. 101
9. The McRae Papers, Huse to Crenshaw April 14th 1863
10. Ibid, OR Series IV Volume II, pages 543-547
11. Ibid OR, p. 546
12. Ibid OR, p. 556
13. Ibid.OR, p. 893
14. Ibid OR, p. 564
15. Ibid, Wise p. 103.

GENERAL COLIN J McRAE C.S.A

Colin J McRae was born in Sneedsboro, North Carolina on October 22, 1813, his family then moved to Mississippi and after his father's death McRae took over his banking and finance companies in 1835. He then went on to serve a term on the Mississippi legislature. In 1840, McRae moved to Mobile Alabama, and helped set up the cotton trading company Boykin & McRae (later Boykin, McRae & Foster). At the outbreak of war he worked on the defences of Mobile, and helped to establish the Selma, Alabama Arsenal. McRae was an original member of the Confederate congress which was at the time in Montgomery, Alabama, and signed the Constitution of the Provisional Government of Confederate States.

In July, 1862 McRae became an agent in the Confederate Ordnance Bureau. And in 1863 he was sent by the Confederate Government, because of his experience in banking and finance, to Europe to act as the Confederacy's Chief Financial Agent for the Erlanger loan. He arrived in England on May 13, 1863, aged 50, to oversee Confederate financial policy in Europe. His first mission was to put in place a system of credit so the Confederacy could continue their purchasing of foreign goods. (1) At that time the financial stability of the Confederacy was in jeopardy from questionable record keeping and a lack of financial oversight. He proceeded to Paris to work with John Slidell on the Erlanger loan. Some complaints made to Richmond about Confederate Ordnance Department purchasing agent Caleb Huse resulted in an investigation by McRae into the matter, which turned out to be quite lengthy, taking until October 1864 to conclude.

After the Civil War ended, Colin McRae remained in Britain to close out the business dealings of the former Confederate States of America, as well as cooperate with a United States Government investigation into his handling of Confederate finances. The US Government suspected there was

Confederate money stashed away somewhere, but it all came to nothing. (2)

Perhaps the most interesting thing about Colin McRae is his life after the US Civil War came to an end. McRae was facing prosecution for his role as Chief Financial Agent of the Confederacy and found it prudent to seek domicile on foreign soil, as did some others including Judah Benjamin (London). The Confederate Settlements in British Honduras are a cultural and ethnic sub-group in Belize formerly known as the colony of British Honduras. They are the descendants of Confederates who fled there with their families during and after the US Civil War. They set up several communities, including one called New Richmond. (3)

As the American Civil War erupted, colonial leaders in the British Honduras saw an opportunity to profit from the sale of war materiel to the new Confederate States. Soon a profitable trade in supplies to Confederate America boosted the colonial economy and British Honduras became receptive to the Confederate cause. The colonial governor and other officials were also interested in recruiting Southern planters who were knowledgeable in growing sugar and cotton and they were offered substantial subsidies and tax exemptions to relocate there. Post-bellum, Robert E. Lee, Jefferson Davis and others repeatedly advised Southerners not to flee to British Honduras but the prospect of establishing a new plantation economy in the colony proved very tempting. A small number of Alabama, Louisiana and Mississippi plantation owners who took the colonial governor of British Honduras' offers of land at a reduced price were wanted by American authorities for various crimes, and others had simply lost everything during the war or through Federal property taxation policies during Reconstruction. (4) Still others who served the Confederacy overseas just knew better than to come back to America. Evidence suggests while Brazil was a popular place to relocate, more Confederates initially fled to British Honduras than any other destination, in part because they could easily acclimatize to the English speaking colony. One of the most famous ex-Confederates who went to New Richmond, British Honduras post-bellum was Colin J. McRae, the former Chief Financial Agent in Europe. (5) Never officially pardoned after the war, he elected to run his plantation and mercantile business from a safe distance, arriving there in 1867. He also ran a cattle plantation and mahogany business with Joseph Benjamin (brother of Judah Benjamin) as his partner.

Upon his death in 1877, McRae was the last remaining resident of New Richmond, and his estate passed to his sister Catherine until his nieces and nephews from another sister were of age. It is unknown when exactly his extensive collection of business papers came to America, but in 2003 they were discovered in the attic of the Kate Shepherd house in Mobile, Alabama. They were acquired from the owners by the South Carolina Confederate Relic Room and Military Museum in 2006, and after returning from a conservation lab, they are archived and housed at the SCCRRMM. The Caleb Huse Audit Series of the McRae Papers is comprised of seventeen sub-series. The series reflects the scope of his business dealings for the Confederate Government from 1861 through to July 1863, particularly with one particular commission house. These papers were mainly gathered by Colin McRae and his assistant, M. Hildreth Bloodgood for the investigation into Huse, but also the legitimacy of the S. Isaac, Campbell & Company book keeping practices. The S. Isaac, Campbell & Co. sub-series is the largest, containing 305 documents stretching from August 12, 1861 through December 31, 1863. (6)

NOTES:

1. South Carolina Confederate Relic Room and Military Museum, *Colin McRae Business Papers*, series II.
2. Simmons, Donald C. *Confederate Settlements in British Honduras*, McFarland and Company Publishers, 2001, p. 121
3. Simmons, Donald C. *New Richmond: The City that was to Equal its Namesake,* Belize Magazine, Volume I, 2004.
4. Ibid, Simmons, p. 5
5. Ibid, Simmons, p. 16, Ex-president Jefferson Davis wrote a personal note to McRae expressing his disappointment with his decision to leave England and settle in the British Honduras. McRae's brother (John) who was Governor of Mississippi also wrote him along the same lines. In fact, John McRae died during a visit to his brother at his New Richmond plantation in 1868. See also: Dunn, William *The Lost Confederates* Detroit News Magazine, December 13, 1978. Estimates of CS immigration to the Honduras vary from 2,000 to 7,800 from 1866 to 1870. For whatever reason, the Brazil Confederado settlements proved more successful in the long run than those in the malarial British colony.
6. Ibid, SCCRRMM: Colin McRae Papers.

DISPATCHING COLIN McRAE TO LONDON & THE DELAYED ARRIVAL OF M. HILDRETH BLOODGOOD

By mid-1863, the Isaacs' commission house had filled contracts with the Confederate Government for close to 185,000 P-53 Enfield rifles, army shoes, boots, trousers, jackets, wool cloth, knapsacks, blankets, accoutrement kits, cooking kits and almost everything else imaginable, in some cases advancing funds on deposit. As a result, with the cotton loan now in place, SIC & Co presented their sizeable bill to Erlanger & Co, and made the following agreement for payments of sums due (1):

"*Copy of agreement between Messrs. S. Isaac, Campbell & Co. and Messrs. Emile Erlanger & Co.*
LONDON, May 25, 1863.
We, the undersigned, Isaac, Campbell & Co., of London, and Emile Erlanger & Co., of Paris, have made today the following agreement on behalf of the claim Isaac, Campbell & Co. state to have against the Confederate Government for the sum of about £515,000. Major Huse, who incurred this debt with Isaac, Campbell & Co., will give them a certificate of indebtedness for the above sum, which they will hand over to Emile Erlanger & Co. Emile Erlanger & Co. engage to hand over to Isaac, Campbell & Co. £150,000 of paid-up bonds for which they have subscribed, and for which they will credit Emile Erlanger & Co. with £135,000, less the discount allowed to subscribers, this quantity being considered paid up.

Isaac, Campbell & Co. will receive, furthermore, from Emile Erlanger & Co. £150,000 in bonds, the former crediting the latter with £135,000, no discount being allowed to these; £90,000, which Emile Erlanger & Co. have advanced for Isaac, Campbell & Co., £90,000, together with interest,

will be taken over from their account and credited to Emile Erlanger & Co. Emile Erlanger & Co. will pay in cash £40,000 to Isaac, Campbell & Co., and on the 2nd of June the further sum of £20,000; and Isaac, Campbell & Co. will have the right to draw on Emile Erlanger & Co. at ninety days' date for the sum of £40,000, and place this to the credit of the latter, less interest for seventy days.
Emile Erlanger & Co. engage to deliver the above-mentioned £300,000 of bonds as soon as they are ready, and half of these not later than the 15th of June.
Isaac, Campbell & Co. will leave in the hands of Emile Erlanger & Co., to be returned to the Government, the cotton warrants and 8 per cent, bonds now deposited with the latter for the security of their advance of £90,000.
In the event of Isaac, Campbell & Co. wishing to resell these bonds they shall give the refusal of the bonds to Emile Erlanger & Co. at such price offered by other parties and which Isaac, Campbell & Co. are willing to accept.
Isaac, Campbell & Co. remain responsible to the Government for their account, and hold Emile Erlanger & Co. free from any loss or reclamation in this respect; and they furthermore leave the balance of their account as a guarantee, and will not claim it from the Government for two months. Isaac, Campbell & Co. will allow their account to be audited by General McRae or any person he may appoint on his behalf.

EMILE D'ERLANGER,
For EMILE ERLANGER & CO.
S. ISAAC, CAMPBELL & CO."

And according to the terms as stated above, the Isaacs left with a cheque for £40,000, and no doubt an improved opinion of themselves. The firm did not know what was in the works back in Richmond, Virginia, or what was about to be set in motion the next day. The highest officers of the Confederate War Department, after receiving the correspondence of Crenshaw and Major Ferguson, deemed the allegations against Huse worthy of a full investigation. On May 26, 1863 Colin McRae was officially appointed to inspect the business practices of purchasing agent Caleb Huse on the day after SIC & Co made their arrangements with Erlanger & Co. McRae was to pay particular attention to the contracts Huse made with SIC & Co, as this is where the allegations of impropriety resided. Arriving in London, Colin McRae then set up his office at the Burlington Hotel in Cork Street London. McRae wrote to Caleb Huse on July 22nd, 1863, the following note announcing his intentions:

"I am in receipt of a communication from Col J Gorgas, Chief of Ordnance, informing me that I have been appointed to examine your accounts as the disbursing officer of the War Department abroad. Please let me know when and where you will have your accounts ready to place before me. At any time after the 1st August I shall be ready to commence the investigation." (2)

Huse for his part welcomed the audit, hopeful for a complete, prompt exoneration and with it the return of his reputation. He was blissfully unaware that Saul Isaac had been keeping two sets of accounts, and that the Confederacy had been systematically overcharged for virtually every item purchased over the past two years. Colin McRae was primarily in charge of overseeing the Erlanger loan; a full time job in and of itself. The potentially scandalous matter with Huse was an unpleasant sidebar to his main mission. And McRae soon received additional unwelcome news that M. Hildreth Bloodgood had been appointed to assist in the examination, and that McRae ought to await his arrival before proceeding with an examination of Huse and SIC & Co's books. Secretary James Seddon wrote to Bloodgood five days after appointing McRae on June 1, 1863:

"...The Department hereby authorises you to examine the accounts of Major Caleb Huse of the Ordnance Department. The appointment is made subject to the following instruction: Some short time ago the Chief of Ordnance applied on behalf of Major Huse the appointment of a person for the examination of his vouchers and accounts. I suggested the name of General CJ McRae as a suitable person for the purpose, this was acceded to and have communicated with him. It is supposed that Gen McRae may be otherwise employed and may not be able to give all the attention necessary. Therefore the Department has concluded to approach you in the hope, and in the event that General McRae cannot act or is unable to do so you are hereby authorised to do so alone....The Department prefer that General McRae and yourself should act together and you will therefore communicate with him on your arrival." (3)

The wording was polite but the message was clear enough. The audit would not proceed until the undetermined future arrival of M. Hildreth Bloodgood, who for his part apparently felt no particular reason to rush to London to expedite the matter. Whether this was intentional or not on the part of Secretary of War Seddon, Huse felt anxious about the delays and on July 24, 1863, worried by the lack of progress into his case, he wrote directly to McRae:

"A letter received from Col Gorgas by me yesterday on the subject of my accounts appears to be more full than the one which you received by the same conveyance, and which is referred to in your note of yesterday. I therefore inclose (sic) a copy of it. Mr Bloodgood has not arrived, and it being uncertain when he may be expected, and really important, as I conceive, that as early an examination as possible should be made, I beg to suggest that you request some other gentleman from the Confederate States to discharge the duty expected by the War Department of Mr Bloodgood. I am only desirous that the examination should be made as soon as practicable, and in view of the effect that the charges brought against me by Major Ferguson in his letter to you may have in lessening the confidence of business man in me until these charges are found to be untrue, it seems to me highly important for the interest of the government that the examination should be made as promptly and as thoroughly as possible. As matters now stand, important business negotiations may at any time be interrupted by interested parties circulating the story that I am an officer under charges of malfeasance in office. An attempt of this kind has already been made, as you are aware, by William G Crenshaw. I beg, therefore, both as a matter of public importance and private interest to myself, that you will take steps for having at least a preliminary examination made at an early day."

Regardless of the sentiments expressed by Caleb Huse, matters involving the examination were held up by the continued non-appearance of M. Hildreth Bloodgood and would be for a couple more months. Finally, the following note announcing his arrival was sent to Colin McRae. Bloodgood was a gentleman known to enjoy the genteel watering holes of Leamington Spa in Warwickshire during his time in Britain. (4) Still in no particular hurry and as if on holiday, he wrote the following memorandum to McRae back in London, from his location at a hotel resort announcing his arrival, dated August 28, 1863:

*"Regent Hotel, Leamington Spa
Dear Sir,
I arrived yesterday per steamer (from Havanna) (sic) at Southampton. I enclose you a letter which will explain itself. As I understand it, it is for you to decide whether my services are needed and if so what shape they are." (5)*

If Bloodgood's memo to McRae is correct, he arrived at the south coast of England (Southampton) and instead of travelling in the direction of London to meet McRae, he headed north to the spas at Warwickshire which were 78 miles away. That brief but newsy dispatch from Bloodgood in Leamington Spa had still not made it to McRae by September 4, 1863, a week later. With the pattern of delay continuing, McRae posted the following correspondence to Colonel Josiah Gorgas on that same date:

"Having been much engaged during the past week with other business, I have made but little progress in examining the accounts of Major Huse, and as Mr Bloodgood has now arrived in England I shall ask his assistance before proceeding with the work. Mr Bloodgood has not yet been to London, nor have I heard directly from him, but have learned that he reached Liverpool on the 28th ultimo. If I do not hear from him by Monday, the 6th, when I will be prepared to go on with the examination of the accounts, I will address him a note asking his assistance." (6)

Reading between the lines, and unless we are missing something, the message from Colin McRae to Gorgas seems clear enough…Where is M.H. Bloodgood and why has he not yet contacted me or been to London yet? On September 15, 1863 McRae, having finally achieved a rendezvous with Bloodgood, again wrote to Colonel J Gorgas with an update on his lack of progress, and seems initially sympathetic to the financial plight of the SIC & Co firm:

"You should be advised of what has been done on this side of the water in reference to the settlement of the account of Major Caleb Huse with Messrs S. Isaac, Campbell & Co. I think that the settlement of this account was very favourable to the government, as it enabled us to dispose of £300,000 of the stock of the (Erlanger) loan at the issue price. But I fear that it will be disastrous to Messrs S. Isaac, Campbell & Co, as they have the whole

of this stock, representing £267,224 15s 10d of their account on hand; also £50,000 in gold in the Confederacy, amounting to an aggregate to £317 224 15s 10d, none of which is available unless they were to force a sale of stock. This would entail a loss of £ 80,000 or $400,000...Great as this sacrifice would be Mr Saul Isaac (the financial partner of the house) informs me that unless they can get early relief from our government they will be compelled to make it, as it will be impossible for them to meet their engagements, with so large an amount locked up in Confederate securities."

McRae wrote in conclusion to this lengthy correspondence, which actually had little of substance to report:

"The result is that this house, which has been so much maligned by our overzealous friends, is likely to be ruined by having trusted our government when nobody else would...I have seen Mr Bloodgood and arranged with him to take up the examination of Major Huse's accounts on the 17th (Sept) instant....we shall avail ourselves of the valuable assistance of Mr H.O Brewer a gentleman of high character and a thorough businessman familiar with all sorts of accounts and devoted to our cause." (7)

McRae was being munificent here, having not yet begun his formal audit he had yet to discover the duplicity of Saul Isaac and SIC & Co. He would change his tune regarding the Isaacs soon enough. The immediate effect of the delays in putting together all the parties necessary for the audit was to place additional pressure on Caleb Huse, and undermine his ability to do the job of a purchasing agent attempting to supply the war effort. Colonel Josiah Gorgas was in the unenviable spot of being stuck in the middle, between the Secretary of War, the Quartermaster's Department (Ferguson and Crenshaw) and his own purchasing agent, Caleb Huse. Whether the delay in arrival on the part of M.H. Bloodgood were intentional (or not), this much is known... The Secretary of War James Seddon had a financial interest with respect to the Crenshaw venture, hence it should not be difficult to see his grim countenance lurking in the background.

NOTES:

1 *War of the Rebellion: A Compilation of the Official Records of the Union and Confederate Armies*, US Government Printing Office, 1902, Series IV, Volume II, p. 888.
2. Bennett, John, *A Popular Place with Rebels*, Crossfire magazine, ACWRT no. 76, April 2005.
3 The McRae Papers: Correspondence from James Seddon to M. H. Bloodgood, June 1, 1863.
4 The McRae Papers, Correspondence of M. H. Bloodgood to Colin McRae August 28, 1863.
5 Ibid, OR Series IV Volume II p.889
6 Ibid, p. 890
7 Ibid, p. 886

THE INVESTIGATION BEGINS

By mid-October 1863, with the belated arrival of M.H. Bloodgood, the investigation of Caleb Huse and his dealings with SIC & Co was finally underway. Previous correspondence between McRae and Seddon clearly established that Bloodgood reported directly to the War Department, not Colin McRae or Josiah Gorgas. (1) This created a potentially awkward working relationship between the parties, since Colin McRae held the rank of General, which made him the ranking officer on site as well as the Confederate Government's chief financial agent in Europe. In effect though, Bloodgood reported to McRae's superior (Seddon), not to him. On October 16th, 1863, Colin McRae wrote the following letter to Major James B. Ferguson, Huse's original accuser, inviting him to present his evidence:

"Sir,
In June last you addressed me a letter making charges against Major Caleb Huse. I replied, referring you to the War Department and enclosed a copy of your letter to Richmond. I have since then, at the Secretary of War's request, undertaken (with the aid of MH Bloodgood) the examination of Major Huse's accounts.
We will be in London for some days and would be glad to hear from you personally if possible, if not by letter with full details of your charges. The former course would be preferable, as having the papers before us we could confer more understandingly. We would ask your immediate attention and aid, as our stay here is but limited, and the Department desires, for many reasons, a thorough examination and a speedy report". (2)

Major Ferguson thoughtfully replied to the questions set out by McRae, sending the following (undated letter) to the attention of Colin McRae and M. Hildreth Bloodgood:

"Answers to questions forwarded by General CJ McRae:

Question 1

WHAT AMOUNT OF COMMISSION AND FROM WHOM RECEIVED?
I answer to the foregoing I shall give the substance of a conversation with Major Huse shortly after my arrival. He said on some of his purchases he had received a commission. I explained my surprise that he should have done so, and I expressed the opinion that the amount of commission should have been deducted from the face of the invoice in the shape of a discount. He said that it was the way of some of the brokers to divide with parties giving them orders as part of their commission. He also stated that he intended to pay his travelling expenses and the balance amounting of £1000 or so he intended to use in purchasing a military library to be given to the Ordnance Department. I ask that the evidence of the Hon J Mason and Capt North of the Navy Dept to be taken on this point.

Question 2

WHAT EVIDENCE HAVE YOU OF THIS SPECIFICATION?
WHAT GOODS WERE THEN CHANGED IN THIS INVOICE AND WHAT PROOF HAVE YOU ON THE FACT?
In reference to the first specification to my charge No 2 suspecting goods sent out by "Justitia" charged at 40% or 50 % above the market price of the day. I submit the following. In looking over the invoice of the above mentioned goods my attention was particularly struck with an item of 12,000 yards of blue grey army cloth charged at 7/6 per yard at a commission of 2 1/2 %. I took a sample from a piece of cloth which Maj Huse informed me was the same kind as sent out by the "Justitia". I submitted the sample to several highly respectable manufacturers I asked them at what price they would make a similar cloth.
I now submit copies of their written tenders, also various other samples of my own purchases with prices attached which I think will prove to you the truth in charge of this specification. After stating the foregoing I asked to be furnished with the invoice of the "Justitia" as handed to me by Mr Bloodgood is not a correct copy of the invoice exhibited to me by Maj Huse last December, the commission is left out... In further proof of which, I beg you will swear Mr Thomas Bayne, who was present with me at the

*office of S. Isaac, Campbell & Co where this invoice was exhibited. I ask that Mr W Crenshaw and Mr Charles Hobson be sworn on the subject of commission.
Your obedient servant,
Maj JB Ferguson."* (3)

On the issue of Question 1, or the commission paid to Caleb Huse, Major Ferguson referenced a letter from CS Navy Commander James North, who in late April, 1863 wrote to the Major to share a personal experience with SIC & Co that reads like a deposition: *"...That I did call on S. Isaac...and that Mr. Isaac did in the course of conversation make an offer to split with me a commission of 5 per cent on a business transaction for the Confederate Government and that I did regard that offer as an attempt to induce me to enter into a transaction to defraud the Confederate Government, and that I did reject the same on those grounds."*

Kudos to Commander North for his hindsight and additionally for taking the high moral ground two years after Caleb Huse arrived in London to find the business of purchasing military supplies a quagmire. With due diligence and dispatch Huse appears to have made his initial contracts with SIC & Co in good faith, in the best interest of his country which at that time was in their hour of greatest need. The circumstances in 1863 lacked the same degree of desperation and anxiety of mid-1861, and there were other sources available for purchasing agents by that time. It was easier to turn down an offer when other options exist. The issue was not the commission (a fact admitted by Huse), but rather, was Huse complicit with the Isaacs in defrauding the Confederate Government through systematically overcharging for supplies?

Colin McRae was forced to admit difficulties in the examination in a letter to Seddon on October 23rd 1863. He wrote (in part):

"Since my last of September 15th to Col Gorgas, Mr Bloodgood and myself have spent much time upon these accounts and yet have not been able to make an examination complete enough to report to you our final conclusions. We are both here in London, and have made arrangements with an accounting and examining house which I think will enable us to arrive at nearly certain conclusions. Major Huse has shown from the very first every desire to aid us in every way in his power. My object is simply

to report the fact that we are at work and making as much progress as the enormous and complicated nature of the transactions admit, and will, at as early a day as practicable, send you an official report".(4)

Caleb Huse himself on the following day, October 24th, in his efforts to aid the enquiry as described in the above letter, offered the books of S. Isaac, Campbell & Co for examination. At least the one set of books of which he knew existed, in the following correspondence to McRae and Bloodgood he explained:

"The charges against me appear to be limited to my transactions with the house of S. Isaac, Campbell & Co. It has been assumed that no one could be sufficiently well acquainted with the miscellaneous articles embraced in my purchases of and through that house to make the purchases understandingly, and that I have therefore placed myself completely in the power of that house, perhaps innocently, but at all events to the prejudice of the interests of the Confederate States Government. When this investigation first commenced I foresaw great difficulty in the way of making it thorough, which I was very anxious it should be, and expressed my anxiety to Messrs S. Isaac, Campbell & Co, at the same time that I furnished them a copy of Major Ferguson's letter to Mr McRae, denouncing me as a dishonest agent of the government. They appreciated the difficulties of the case, and expressed themselves desirous of doing anything in their power to enable me to vindicate my character. They have offered to exhibit their books to the auditors appointed by the Confederate States Government to examine my accounts, and to give them the means of tracing every transaction they have had with me from the date of my first order, not only for goods purchased by them on my order, but for everything sold to me from their own establishment. My collection of samples has been made entirely for my own guidance. Not expecting such an examination as this now going on. I find that it will be impossible for me to provide you with samples of every lot of articles purchased, and to state accurately the price and date of purchases as you desire. With some articles this can be done, with others it cannot. Some articles have been purchased by S. Isaac, Campbell & Co, in small lots as they could get them. In such cases I have only preserved samples of lots, which differed considerably either in price or quality, or both. You will perceive, therefore, that while my collection of samples is quite sufficient for the purpose intended, and is indeed serviceable than

it would be if the samples were more numerous, it is not adapted to the purpose for which you desire to make use of it.

I beg therefore to suggest to you as the only really efficient means of arriving at the facts you wish to ascertain, that you will avail yourselves of the first offer made by S. Isaac, Campbell & Co, and carefully examine their books. In the course of such an examination you would be able to determine the actual profit made by S. Isaac, Campbell & Co, on every article, and you could afterward, if you should think proper, continue your examination by applying to the houses from which S. Isaac, Campbell & Co made their purchases, the names and addresses of which you could learn from the invoice book of Messrs S. Isaac, Campbell & Co." (5)

The broadness of the charges made by Ferguson and Crenshaw presented considerable difficulty for the auditors in terms of either dismissal or validation since the items purchased by Huse over the past two years were long gone presumably sub-serving the cause of the Confederacy on the battlefields of the American South. As a result these goods were not available for the auditors' inspection or comparison as to their quality. Most importantly, Huse himself provided the auditors a new direction with the suggestion to ...*continue your examination by applying to the houses from S. Isaac, Campbell & Co made their purchases...* (6) Would the purchase orders of sellers match the selling price to the Confederacy? Were there two sets of invoices? The investigation was still full of loose ends in December 1863, and with the year closing fast, very little progress had been made by McRae and Bloodgood toward resolution of the matters at hand. And with SIC & Co.'s continual denials of any wrongdoing, McRae wrote to Saul Isaac with a sense of frustration, to ask for further evidence on December 11, 1863:

"A letter of the 25th inst to me which was intended as a reply to Major Ferguson's charges by more denials...It would be much better if you could sustain your denials by some corroborating testimony. I have therefore returned your letter of the 25th November with the paper accompanying it. I think it proper to sustain your statements by other testimony" (7)

Say what you will about the character of the Isaacs, as men of business they proved themselves time and again to be very tough to corner under examination. The British Commission could not do much with either Saul or Samuel Isaac in terms of generating an admission against interest (8) in the Weedon Bec affair, much less arrive to the truth of the matter. In the end they were happy to merely cancel their contract. And likewise, McRae was getting nowhere with SIC & Co as far as the charges made against Huse. Back in Richmond, the Secretary of War, James A. Seddon wrote expressing his irritation on December 29, 1863, as follows:

"I learn with less surprise than regret, of the discoveries which have been made in the examination of accounts of Messrs S. Isaac, Campbell & Co with Major Huse. For some time I have had strong suspicions that the practices of that firm were more sharp than honest, and that Major Huse, through overconfidence or some other motive, was allowing the interests of the dept to suffer in his transactions with them.
It was fortunate that you took the measure of calling in a public accountant to examine the books of this firm. They had evidently expected, by the appearance of great fairness and the proffer of every facility, to induce yourself and your assistants to take their accounts, on very cursory inspection, as satisfactory.
They had no idea from the very first of submitting them to the observation of a practical accountant, versed in the shipping ways of mercantile usage, where false invoices and deceptive accounts are regular matters of trade. This firm have manifestly changed their whole face of proceedings, and, from an attempt to blind you into overconfidence, are now seeking, by effrontery and concealment, to obtain all possible advantages. The pretences asserted for discounts and commissions can certainly not be countenanced by English justice or mercantile honor, and while you may have difficulty in ferreting out the truth, so far as you do succeed you have only to be firm in your demands, and the dread of exposure will compel their ready compliance."(9)

Seddon is, of course, on the right track except for the last sentence about *the dread of exposure* compelling the *ready compliance* of the Isaacs. They were already very widely known as dishonest businessmen (sharpers) prone to cooking the books. Even so, those two proved too tough a nut for the Confederate auditors to crack. In reply to this letter by Seddon, Colin McRae gave himself the luxury of time before he composed a diplomatic reply on February 19, 1864:

"I note your remarks relative to Major Huse, I am hardly ready at this moment to express final opinion, but I deem it due to him to say that although he has made serious mistakes, I think there is no good reason to suspect his integrity, and that he has always sought what seemed in the best interests of the Government, and has with all his mistakes really been of great service and done great good, and that you should take into consideration the immense labours which he has been compelled to discharge almost singly, and which forced him to place great confidence in some leading house, which was unfortunately, as you surmise, much misplaced in the case of S. Isaac, Campbell & Co, but I can see no reason to believe there has been any collusion between them. In confirmation of the above views I inclose (sic) you letters from Hon John Slidell and Emile V Erlanger, which you will perceive do not agree with the charges of extravagance against him; and I will further add that these opinions are, I believe, concurred in by leading houses with whom he has dealt, and by the accountants examining his accounts." (10)

As M Hildreth Bloodgood had spent more time on the investigation than thought Gorgas intervened on his behalf insisting that he be paid the same as a Captain of Artillery, which was granted by Seddon, and backdated to September 1, 1862. This suggests though that whatever his whereabouts prior to that date, he was not on government business. Huse, still intent on vindication, again wrote to McRae (and Bloodgood) on February 26th, 1864, the following:

"I have the honor herewith to enclose a copy of a letter and statement from Messrs Quilter Ball & Co – (An accounting firm acting on behalf of the CS Govt) re S. Isaac, Campbell & Co's account. Also a copy of my letter to SIC & Co the former dated Feb 20th and the latter Feb 26th. Mr Quilter informs me that they are prepared to submit to you an opinion concerning my accounts generally and he suggests that they should do so, without waiting for the final action of SIC & Co, although he thinks with me that they are most likely to long delay a settlement on any terms that I may agree to." (11)

Being old hands at questionable financial dealings but sensing their time running out, SIC & Co became more aggressive in their attempts to re-establish themselves with their former big customer, the British military.

Their grassroots effort in the form of an extraordinary memo from May 1863 reveals the firm's desperation.

"This was circulated by noted military outfitters ISAAC, CAMPBELL & COMPANY to restore their business with the British government. Dated London May, 1863; addressed:

TO THE OFFICER COMMANDING. Sent to the C.O. of every British regiment denouncing the Secy of War's intention of the government to supply all [British] regts with accessories and to make those accessories themselves hence cutting-out all contractors…as unjust to the Army and contractors [who] for years devoted energies to this business. Offers lengthy details and Campbell's plaintive plea of having worked 40 years to…benefit the soldier… and introduced improvements in uniforms, reduced prices, endeavoured to add to his comfort…[etc.]. The letter requests all regiments to immediately send a payment for all invoices still due… thanks them for many years of business relations and expresses regrets at the present situation, asking for letters of recommendation as well as help in changing the unjust and critical ruling."

Interestingly, found in the McRae papers are several replies to this call to arms. Colin McRae may have collected these letters to lend some support to the previous good character of SIC & Co in their business dealings with the British army. Perhaps the Isaacs' treachery was just terribly misunderstood, after all. Actually, all these endorsements prove is that not even the Isaacs were habitually dishonest all the time. And it brings to mind the famous old saying about human nature: The more he spoke of his honour, the faster we counted our spoons.(12)

Two examples of these letters of endorsement follow:

"No 296 of 1863
Camp Curragh
June 5 1863
Gentlemen
In reply to your letter dated May 18th 1863 I have the pleasure to state that I have always been perfectly satisfied with the quality of supplies furnished by you to this battalion, and your business relations have met with my entire approval.
HL Longden, Col Comm 10th Foot." (13)

And the second endorsement, this one from a regiment stationed in India:

"No 186 of 1863
Poonah
July 22nd 1863
Gentlemen
I have the honour to acknowledge the receipt of your letter of the 18th May 1863 and at your decline in consequence of Government (not clear). To confirm the supply of regimental necessities to the battalion under my command.
I cannot close transactions with your firm without expressing my entire satisfaction, and I believe that of my predecessor at the manner in which your business has been conducted, and in the quality of all supplies furnished during now nearly five and twenty years, with only an interruption of a few months.
I have the honour to be Gentlemen, your obedient servant
Signed W Wilby
Lt Col Comm (unclear)" (14)

Considering how gracious these British Officers were in their letters of support to SIC & Co, one assumes they were splitting commissions as well, this being the business practice of the day. To wit, if these were considered improper payments, these officers were never knowingly prosecuted. The British army for their part seemed content to put their past business dealings with the Isaacs in their rear view mirror, and move on. The weight of evidence *en toto* supports only one logical conclusion. The business philosophy of SIC & Co might best be summarized with the following, *"Honesty is for the most part less profitable than dishonesty."* (15) This pattern of dishonest dealing from the firm of SIC & Co appeared to be their longstanding practice. If perhaps their duplicity was just being discovered by the CS auditors, it was well known to others in the trade. It is difficult to believe that Huse had no idea of the firm's reputation, but same as in the Weedon Bec scandal, there was a lack of direct evidence that he did. Huse certainly seemed a resolute purchasing agent otherwise, and cooperated fully with the investigation by McRae and Bloodgood. As far as the Isaacs, as the French say, *"plus ça change, plus c'est le même chose"* which means that the more things change, the more they remain the same. The day of reckoning was near for SIC & Co, and Colin McRae would ultimately have to confront the Isaacs directly to reconcile their bill and reduce any payment to offset their overcharges.

NOTES:

1. *War of the Rebellion: A Compilation of the Official Records of the Union and Confederate Armies,* US Government Printing Office, 1902, Series IV, Volume II, p. 888. Note: Secretary of War Seddon makes it very clear to McRae that M.H. Bloodgood reports not to him, or Gorgas, but the War Department (Seddon).
2. Ibid, OR Series IV Volume II p 892
3. *Colin J. McRae Collection (1861 to 1872),* South Carolina Confederate Relic Room and Military Museum Archives, Huse Audit Series: Letter from Major James B. Ferguson to Colin McRae (undated).
4. OR Series IV Volume II p885.
5. Depending on your point of view, either Huse got lucky with that suggestion, or else he knew more of the Isaacs' business practices than he was letting on previously...probably the latter.
6. Ibid, OR Series IV Volume II p. 894
7. An *'admission against interest'* is a legal term, which aside from its *prima facie* meaning of making a statement of truth that is damaging to the person making it, an *admission against interest* has the additional component of being admissible as an exception to the *hearsay rule* in the event of a lawsuit in Federal court. In Britain, which differs from American Law on this point, *hearsay* was admissible in civil matters, primarily to maintain that statements made prior to filing suit were consistent with statements made under oath during trial. Either way, the Isaacs were never naïve enough to fall into this sort of trap.
8. Ibid, McRae Papers (CJ McRae to Saul Isaac Dec 11, 1863)
9. Ibid.
10. OR Series IV Volume II p 1067
11. Ibid p. 154
12. Boswell, James, *The Life of Samuel Johnson* (1791), p. 123, as follows: *"But if he does really think that there is no distinction between virtue and vice, why, Sir, when he leaves our houses let us count our spoons."*
13. The 10th Regiment of Foot did service in the first American War of Independence during the 1770s. In fairness, it would appear the Colonel of this Regiment would have some level of credibility.

14. Ibid, OR Series IV Volume II.
15. The philosopher Plato (428 BCE to 348 BCE) is credited with this astute observation.

HUSE FINALLY CLEARED

As the year 1863 ended and 1864 came in, and with no resolution of the charges against him on the horizon, Caleb Huse fretted about his sullied reputation but continued his duties as purchasing agent for the CS Ordnance Department. During the year 1864, despite some setbacks on the battlefields of the American South, the Erlanger bonds actually increased slightly in value. *The London Times* as late as September 1864 reported the holders of Erlanger bonds were better off than with Federal securities. (1) As a result, with their cotton loan still in good standing, even though it was overdrawn to the tune £200,000 in February 1864, the Confederate purchasing agents were still shipping provisions to the South virtually up until the ports of Charleston, South Carolina and Wilmington, North Carolina fell a year later. (2) However, with the outcome of the McRae investigation into Caleb Huse and the SIC & Co overcharges still pending, less and less business was transacted through the Isaacs' commission house.

Finally, on March 12, 1864, after almost a year had passed since the allegations were first made, the Assistant Secretary of War James Campbell wrote:

...all the communications from Messrs McRae and Bloodgood official and unofficial acquit Maj Huse of any charge of intentional error, and of any malfeasance of any kind, and testify to his zeal, energy, and personal honor." (3)

McRae and Bloodgood wrote to Seddon explaining of their conclusions on October 1st 1864:
"We have had no answer from you to our dispatch of March 17, but we understand from Major Huse that he has received from home an official communication endorsing his conduct. It was not our intention in that dispatch to clear him from blame, but to relieve him from any charge of

collusion, and to place before you the difficulties he had to encounter, and the good he has done and tried to do as palliative or offsets against his errors and mistakes. We wished to keep from speaking too severely of his mistakes, because of the difficulties of his position, but not to endorse or overlook them". (4)

By July 1864, well over a year later, it was also found that S. Isaac, Campbell & Co had kept two sets of books, one showing the actual costs of the goods purchased, and the other showing the prices the firm charged the Confederate Government. As might be expected, the Isaacs thought their adding a slight premium to their cost was justified, and were not receptive to the notion of refunding any of it. Colin McRae in a letter to Secretary of War James Seddon on July 4th, 1864 wrote as follows:

"Not being able to come to a settlement in any other way on the proposition of Messrs S.I.C. & Co, we have agreed to leave the matter to arbitration, provided there be but one arbitrator, and he be a barrister or attorney of eminence. The papers are now in the hands of our solicitors, Messrs Thomas & Hollams, who with the solicitors of S.I.C. & Co are to select the barrister." (5) The following letter confirms the above statement by McRae, Thomas and Hollams were part of the Quilter and Ball firm who Caleb Huse used to verify his accounts.

"London 3rd August 1864.
Dear Sirs,
Isaac, Campbell & Co v Confederate States:
Referring to our interview of this morning we do not gather that the (illegible) initiated by Maj Huse and Messrs Isaac Campbell & Co was intended as anything more than the basis of a settlement and consequently that it cannot be relied upon as a concluded agreement putting an end to all questions. Assuming this to be the only alternative seems to be to proceed with the arbitration. It is to that our opinion remains unchanged namely that it is practically useless and it would be unwise to attempt to limit the claims of Messrs Isaac Campbell & Co & that of the representatives of the Confederate States of America to agree to an arbitration. The only course is to leave Messrs Isaac, Campbell & Co unfettered as to the demands which they make and to trust to the good sense and discretion of the arbitration as to be made in which we will deal with any attempts which they may

make to depart from accounts and claims already ventured. Of course, the Confederate Govt are in no way legally bound to submit any matters to arbitration, nor can they be sued in this country.
Consequently they have it in their power if they choose to avail themselves of their position wholly to defeat any attempt on the part of Messrs Isaac, Campbell & Co to enforce their demands as Messrs Isaac, Campbell & Co are perhaps not unreasonably pressing for a definite reply.
We shall be glad to receive instructions whether or not we shall proceed with the proposed arbitration and prepare the draft of agreement of reference.
Yours Faithfully
Thomas & Hollams
Messrs Quilter & Ball & Co" (6)

On October 1st, 1864, McRae and Bloodgood wrote again to Secretary of War James A. Seddon:

"Our last letter of July 7, advising you that an arbitration had been ordered relative to the accounts of Messrs Isaac, Campbell & Co, and that an adjourned interview between Mr McRae and Mr Saul Isaac was to take place the following week. We have now to add that the interview was without favourable result, as was also a preliminary arrangement entered into between Mr Isaac and Major Huse, which the latter thought would lead to a settlement on terms which we could approve. These efforts to settle by compromise have resulted only in a loss of time, and the solicitors have been instructed to proceed with the arbitration without further delay. The general holiday enjoyed by gentlemen in the legal profession in England during the months of August and September has prevented any further progress being made to this date.

In the same letter, McRae and Bloodgood then went on to comment on Caleb Huse, even going so far as to suggest a raise in pay for him. The Assistant Secretary of War J. A. Campbell, was having none of it, and responded as follows:

"The correspondence of Messrs McRae and Bloodgood acquitted Major Huse of intentional error and malfeasance, and testified to his zeal, energy, and honor in April last. But the papers since the date of the letter, while exonerating Major Huse from any criminality or dishonor, diminish

materially the character given to him as an efficient and capable officer. They attribute to his failure to give notices and to his facility in his dealings with S. Isaac, Campbell & Co large losses, and their estimate is that his merits and demerits being considered, that upon the whole he is not subject for severe censure. My endorsement was made upon early reports and correspondence, and I have been advised that in the progress of the investigation their judgement has been modified". (7)

Nonetheless Josiah Gorgas was still totally committed to Huse, due to the remarkable work he had already done in the past three years, not just for the Ordnance Department, but more specifically for the Quartermaster's Department, even though he was not specified to do so. While his usefulness with the Quartermaster Department came to an end in May 1863, Huse was ordered to carry on purchasing for other departments, which Gorgas commented on in a letter to Seddon on May 22^{nd,} 1863:

"He (Huse) has, however, declared his unfeigned regret at having volunteered to do service for the Quartermaster's Department to which he was induced by his sense of the nakedness of our army. He has, since the expression of his own wishes on this point, been formally directed to confine his purchases to the Ordnance and Medical Departments, Dr Moore having full confidence in his judgment". (8)

Caleb Huse carried on purchasing for Josiah Gorgas and the Ordnance Department, as well as the Medical Department to the extent his authority permitted, right up until the war ended.

Although legal wrangling carried on until December 1864, SIC & Co's direct dealings with the Confederacy were at an end. SIC & Co invoices from 1863 show that compared to previous years, only a trickle of supplies shipped out to the Confederacy after Colin McRae arrived.

SIC & Co Invoices 1863:

11th April 1863, For Medical Dept Medical & Medicine books
12th May 1863, Bought of W&W Webster £266 worth of books
Oct 22nd 63, 16 Bales of Humnals (sic...Hymnals)
Oct 23rd 63, 1 Piece of blue grey cloth 58 ½ yards

Oct 27th 63, 3,000 Enfield Rifles
750 nipple wrenches
150 bullet moulds
Nov 12th 1863 30 Bales lined Tarpaulin

One invoice dated June 30, 1863 would benefit from further discussion:
28,389 Austrian Rifles
28,389 Bullet Moulds
28,400 Scabbards

Costing £100,284,17s,6d.

These were invoiced per order of Major Huse and bought of S. Isaac, Campbell & Co. The Austrian Rifles from the June 30, 1863 invoice were to ship on the steamer *Miriam* from Hamburg to Bermuda. Huse had previously bought 27,000 M-1854 Austrian Rifles, known now simply as the Lorenz just before the end of 1862, but the Austrian arms of that shipment were in a different gauge (calibre) than the .577 Enfield, meaning that non-standard ammunition was required. A variety of other complaints were made about the M-1854 Austrian Rifles, many of which were second hand, and available because the Austrian Government was replacing them with a newer design. (9) In addition, the M-1854 was a weapon that may have been more easily understood had the Confederacy purchased and translated the manual for it, *"Osterrichische Infanterie - Feurgewehr, Wien", 1857*. The bore diameters on M-1854 Austrian Rifles varied with different samples noted in .556, .57, .577, .58 and .59 calibre(s). A valid reason for the mixed report card on this weapon is that ammunition incorrectly sized was issued for it. For example, the original calibre of the Austrian Rifle was 13.9 mm, believed by the Confederate purchasers to be .54. If so, then the Ordnance Department could easily supply the same ammunition currently issued for the US 1841 Mississippi Rifle also in .54. The Austrian Rifle is actually .556 and the Mississippi Rifle ammunition is actually .535. Even though that is only a few hundreds of an inch off from .556, this windage was enough to prevent the bullet from compressing against the grooves in the barrel, effectively making the Austrian Rifle about as accurate as a smoothbore musket. Lastly, the vast majority (about 80%) of the Austrian Rifles came with block sights dead on at 300 schritt', which is the Austrian equivalent of a yard. However, a schritt' is one pace and 300 schritt' is only 225 yards. The *"Osterrichische*

Infanterie - Feur-gewehr, Wien", 1857, explains all this and how to use the fixed sights to hit a target at various distances over or under a distance of 300 schritt.' The later shipment of Austrian Rifles bought by Caleb Huse and purchased from M. Louis Merton was brokered by SIC & Co. Many of the M-1854 Austrian Rifles were classified as second class weapons.

By mid-1863, Major James B Ferguson had taken over all Quartermaster Departmental purchasing from Huse, and he moved north to Manchester to be nearer the wool and cotton mills in Lancashire and Yorkshire.

Samuel and Saul Isaacs' dealings with the Confederacy did not end there, indirectly and unbeknown to the Confederate Government, the Isaac brothers continued to sell goods to the South. In three such transactions in late 1864, Isaacs' former factory in Northampton, which Samuel had leased and later sold to the Turner brothers, provided shirts and Army shoes to Major JF Minter of the Trans Mississippi Department. On November 29, 1864 Turner Bros sold 3,000 pairs of army shoes to Minter, and on December 19, 1864 another 1,400 pairs were purchased. And finally, on an invoice also dated December 19, 1864, 14 bales of grey all wool shirts were brought from Turner Bros. Ironically, these goods were purchased by Major JB Ferguson, the very man who in April 1863, had first bought the allegations of impropriety against Huse and SIC & Co. (10) No doubt the Isaacs overcharged him.
Crenshaw had suffered a personal setback when his factory in Virginia burned down. The Richmond Sentinel, May 16, 1863 reported the following:

"Disastrous Fire. - Soon after 2 o'clock yesterday morning a fire broke out in the extensive factory building of the Crenshaw Woollen company, situated on the south side of the Canal, nearly opposite the foot of 3d street, and spread with such rapidity that the building was destroyed in a short time, together with a portion of the Tredegar Foundry, owned by Anderson & Co., adjoining on the West. The flames lighted up the whole city and the country for miles around. About 3 o'clock the interior portion of the Crenshaw mill, five stories in height, fell with a tremendous crash, leaving the bare brick walls standing. The entire machinery of the mill, together with some manufactured goods, ready for delivery, and doubtless a quantity of un-manufactured stock, were destroyed. The fire was accidental, having, it is believed, to have been caused by friction from the picker, in the rear portion of the mill. This machine was kept going day and night, and it is stated that the man who attended it left the

room for a moment for the purpose of procuring oil, and when he returned the room was in flames."

NOTES:

1. Schwab, John C. *The Confederate States of America*, Yale University Press (1901), p. 36. This Pollyanna-ish attitude on the part of British investors was due to the belief that should the worst come and the CS Government fail, the bonds were secured with bales of cotton, which held an intrinsic value well beyond the amount due on the loans. It never occurred to these investors that the US Treasury Department might not honor the bonds and instead use that cotton to pay down their own crushing war debt.
2. The War of the Rebellion: A Compilation of the Official Records of the Union and Confederate Armies, United States Government Printing Office, (1900) p. 155. Seddon to Colin McRae Feb 12, 1864, ...*the fact is that the loan has already been overdrawn by over £200,000."*
3. Ibid, OR Series IV Volume III, p. 704
4. Ibid, OR Series IV Volume III p 703
5. Ibid, OR, Series IV Volume III, p. 525
6. The McRae Papers
7. Ibid, OR Series IV Volume II p 702/703
8. Ibid, OR Series IV Volume II p 564.
9. Unlike the British Enfields which were virtually all commercially produced, the Austrian Lorenz M-1854s were purchased from the Hapsburg Government. These were largely second hand weapons which were sold to make room for an up-graded model. Some Austrian Rifles were more serviceable than others, and varied lot by lot.
10. Ibid, OR Series IV, Volume II p. 704

S. ISAAC, CAMPBELL & CO: THE END

With the collapse of the Confederacy in May 1865, the company still held £300,000 of Erlanger bonds as part of the agreement between SIC & Co and Erlanger for taking over the company's debt to the Confederate Government. (1) Now that the American Civil War was over these Confederate bonds became next to worthless, the Federal Government would not back them or even release the collateral (cotton) for liquidation by the creditors. The Isaacs, along with a significant number of other European investors in the Erlanger bonds were *raptus regaliter*. (2)

The Isaacs may have at times lacked fidelity, and certainly lacked ethical accounting practices, but they were not quitters. Their arbitration case concerning the Caleb Huse overcharges never reached settlement before the Confederate Government was officially defunct. However, they could and did sue in US Court to recover some of their lost property which failed to run the Union blockade during the war. The case of the captured schooner *Stephen Hart* and the blockade runner *Gertrude* brokered by Speyer and Haywood for S. Isaac, Campbell & Company. The *Stephen Hart* was ostensibly headed for Cuba, but contained military equipage most certainly intended for the Confederate States, via Nassau. The *Stephen Hart* was captured off the coast of Florida on January 29, 1862. This was the last time a vessel using only the wind for locomotion would be used to try to run the blockade…it was too easily caught. The *Gertrude*, a British blockade runner built in Scotland was captured near Eleuthera Island as it headed for Charleston, SC in April 1863. Both were condemned as lawful prize and contraband of war, along with all cargo. The Southern District Court of New York ruled …"it is satisfactorily established that the cargoes of both the *Stephen Hart* and *Gertrude*, were when captured on their way to the enemy's country, into which they were designed to be introduced by a breach of blockade, and as S. Isaac, Campbell & Company was interested in the entire cargo…this inference is regarded as a very proper one and warranted by the proofs invoked." The lawyers for the S. Isaac, Campbell firm had argued the vessel was neutral property and ought to be returned to the rightful owners (themselves). They further argued that the cargo was not intended to be received by belligerents or foreign agents. As evidence, Samuel Isaac's son Henry and brother-in-law Benjamin Hart were domiciled in Nassau, West Indies (Bahamas) as their receiving agents. They were there not as agents of the Confederate Government, but only to conduct the shipping business of the firm. The court rejected the plea and ruled for the US Government as the litigants had not quite come to the bench with *clean hands* based on their well known past activities. (3)

Coming to the bench without clean hands can be used as an affirmative defence in a court of equity. As an equitable defence, it is a bar to recovery, and proved so here. The condemnation was uncontested and no appeal was taken. However, the case of the *Stephen Hart* was more legally ambiguous than the *Gertrude,* in that it was a British-owned commercial schooner captured on the open sea under the flag of a neutral nation (Britain) and was not proven to be bound for any American port, such as the paddle wheeled blockade runner steamship like the *Gertrude.* On that basis, S. Isaac, Campbell & Co. appealed the decision on the *Stephen Hart* and the appeal made it to the United States Supreme Court. It was argued on January 11, 1866, and decided on March 26, 1866.

The failing argument was made by lawyers for S. Isaac, Campbell & Company, as follows: The *Stephen Hart* was a neutral ship flying the Union Jack and Britain was a neutral government. In addition, it was a commercial schooner bound for a neutral destination which was claimed as Cardenas, Cuba. An additional contention was that the Union blockade did not extend to Cuba. All this really meant (in fact) was that the *Stephen Hart* had not yet reached port and the cargo on board had not been conveyed on to a speedier vessel, as with the blockade runner *Gertrude.* Apparently the United States Supreme Court justices were not swayed by that minor distinction either. The *Stephen Hart* was full to the rafters with munitions of war. With a nod to the doctrine of continuous voyage, the US Supreme Court ruled that neutrals who engage in belligerent trade with contraband cargo under the cover of false destination cannot complain if their ships are seized and condemned as enemy property. (4)

The most promising case of the bunch, at least for the Isaacs but also for researchers, seemed to be the *Springbok*. This bark was involved in what appeared to be an illegal seizure on February 23, 1863 about 150 miles off the coast of Nassau. Boarding the vessel, US sailors found the ship under charter by Thomas S. Begbie and carrying a cargo belonging to SIC & Co (both familiar names), but the vessel carried no cargo manifest and based on the unsatisfactory condition of the papers, it was seized. The *Springbok* documents lent insight into the role of SIC & Co silent partner D. Forbes Campbell, discussed elsewhere in this monograph. In addition, a review of the case provides excellent insight into the inner workings of the firm, business associates and the how goods brokered by SIC & Co ran the Union blockade via Nassau. Unlike the *Stephen Hart* or the *Gertrude*, the *Springbok* carried mostly non-contraband with only a small part of its cargo consisting of arms and ammunition. The owners were May & Co, and the Captain one of their sons, James May. The ship had been chartered for the voyage by T.S. Begbie. The charter called for a *"voyage to Nassau with a cargo of lawful merchandise goods, the freight to be paid one half in advance on clearance on the remainder cash on delivery; thirty running days to be allowed for loading at the port...and discharging at Nassau."* (5)

The bills of lading were brokered by Speyer and Haywood, and shipped by Begbie and SIC & Co. The bills of lading did not indicate who the owners were nor did they disclose the contents of more than a third of the packages. The manifest also failed to reveal the nature of the cargo, and both manifest and bills of lading consigned the cargo "to order." No invoices were found on board. A letter from Speyer and Haywood to Captain May instructed the latter to report himself on arrival at Nassau to B. W. Hart who would give him orders as to the delivery of the cargo and any further information required. In the examination *in preparatorio*, (6) the ship's Captain James May stated that he did not know for what reason the *Springbok* had been captured and that he was not aware that there were any contraband goods on board. The prize court ruled his testimony studied ignorance. And so it was decided at the district court level that along with the *Gertrude* and the *Stephen Hart*, the *Springbok* was subject to seizure under a rule of prize court that *"when the same claimants intervene for different vessels or goods...the prize courts inquire, did they come engaged in traffic similar to that which they are charged in that particular case."* (7) In other words, what was their intent? As in the other cases (decided by the same judge) prize courts had to look to see if the claimants came to the bench with "clean hands". It had already been decided in the previous cases that they had not.

In 1863, however, after the decree of condemnation had been issued but before the judgment of the US prize court was delivered, the Isaacs initiated an appeal through the British Government. The Law Officers of the Crown had given it as their opinion that the sentence was unjustifiable both to ship and cargo, but did not intend to do anything about it and in a dispatch to Lord Lyons wrote:

"Her Majesty's Government was therefore disposed to think that the sentence was wrong, and ought to be reversed, but they would nevertheless be glad to see the reasons upon which it was founded, and they would hesitate to instruct your Lordship to interfere in the case until it had been heard before the Court of Appeal...For the above reasons, therefore, and upon a full consideration of the whole case, Her Majesty's Government do not feel that they would be justified, on the materials before them, in making any claim on the United States Government for compensation or damages on behalf of the owners of the cargo of the Springbok." (8)

On appeal, the US Supreme Court in 1866 proved more liberal than the prize court and restored the ship but affirmed the sentence with respect to the cargo, which was worth £66,000. The Chief Justice wrote applying its ruling in the case of the *Bermuda,* it held that "where decision of goods destined ultimately for a belligerent port are being conveyed between two neutral ports by a neutral ship, under a charter made in good faith for that voyage, and without any fraudulent connection on the part of her owners with the ulterior destination of the goods, the ship, though liable to seizure in order to [effect] the confiscation of the goods, is not liable to condemnation as prize". (9)

While trying their separate cases in the US Courts, SIC & Co continued to do a small brokerage business supplying the British Volunteer units and whatever small arms deals around the world they could attract. Overall the business of military arms brokerage was no longer as robust as during the US Civil War, and would not be again. London Armoury had failed in 1866 and reorganized as London Small Arms Co. In 1863 Birmingham Small Arms Trade reorganized into BSA Co. and post-bellum subsisted mostly on government contracts for converting percussion P53s to the Snider breech loading system. And for the SIC & Co firm, in the end burdened by the huge losses from the Erlanger bonds, lacking any great success recovering funds from the US Courts and unable to re-establish any business with the British army, Samuel and Saul Isaac finally admitted defeat. They were declared bankrupt in 1869. The brothers only lasted as long as 1869 due to financial assistance from their supporters in the Hart family. Their legal appeals exhausted, the firm of S. Isaac, Campbell & Co at 71 Jermyn Street, finally folded, resolved to receivers in 1871. Founder Samuel Isaac lost more than his money and his business, SIC & Co, from his dealings with the Confederacy, he had also lost his son, Henry. If Samuel Isaac proved nothing else with his life, he demonstrated an ability to get up again after being knocked down. At the age of 68, he somehow managed to acquire the rights from the promoters of the Mersey Railway Tunnel connecting Liverpool with the Wirral peninsula. He raised the funds to get it completed to great fanfare, and when he passed away shortly afterwards on November 22, 1886, he left an estate valued at £203,084 17s. 9d.

Perhaps the more incredible story is younger brother Saul Isaac, the shady bookkeeper, who served from January 31, 1874 to March 31, 1880 as MP for Nottingham. He was elected to office in the only general election to give Disraeli a parliamentary majority. A little known reference to Saul Isaac being the first Jew of the Conservative party to take his seat in the House of Commons also lends some insight into his business ventures post-SIC & Co. Saul is referenced as an obscure coal merchant from Nottinghamshire. (10) Additional research revealed that in the 1870s, coal was bringing a high price, and there was a prosperous trade in it going on in Nottingham. What better place to find Saul Isaac picking up his fortunes again than in the colliery business?

Saul Isaac's involvement with the colliery comes in the form of two articles in the Jewish Chronicle, the first published on 10th June, 1870 was as follows:

"The new colliery at Clifton, sunk by Sir Robert Clifton, also absorbed a lot of capital. Coal was proved in 1867, and the first sod was cut on 19th June 1868. Sir Robert died shortly after the pit was opened. In May 1870 Saul Isaacs took a lease on the colliery and in June, he announced he would meet all accounts which had occurred prior to his taking possession.

Fortunately for Mr Isaacs, the boom of 1871 – 75 coincided with the pit's period of maximum productivity. The works were completed in June 1871 when Isaacs announced that "a good supply of coal can always be had at the pit bank".(11)

The second article published on 1st July, 1870 stated in part:

"A ceremony of great importance to the local interests of Nottinghamshire has just taken place. Mr Saul Isaac has recently become lessee of the Wilford Bridge and Clifton collieries, with, as the Nottingham Daily Guardian states, the congratulations and goodwill of everybody. Mr Isaac has inaugurated his proprietorship by two splendid entertainments at Nottingham. It may be mentioned that the first shaft was sunk by the late Sir Robert Clifton, MP, whose widow formally opened the colliery on this occasion". (12)

The Isaacs always followed the money where ever it went. The Nottingham Archives show that Saul Isaac (no mention of Samuel) purchased land on September 30, 1871 for £1400 from Henry Smith.(13) And in 1875 he took a lease for land from the Duke of Newcastle as follows: *Lower Soft and Lower or Bottom Hard Seams of coal in closes called King's Meadows in parish of Standard Hill, Nottingham. For 28 years at £450 per annum plus royalty of £75 per acre for Lower Soft and £120 per acre for Bottom Hard coal, plus 1s. for every 2400 lbs. ironstone, but not for unworkable or unmarketable coal.* (14). The National Archives record Saul in and out of court over the years, involved in various lawsuits with banks and business partners. He died in 1903, considerably less well off than his elder brother Samuel, leaving an estate of just £29.00. (15)

NOTES:

1. Business Records of Fraser Trenholm Reel no B/FT 6/19: Liverpool Maritime Museum. *Thomas Greenwood of Leeds was a manufacturer of machinery to produce gun parts. Rowsell Sabine Ripley was a General in the Confederate Army. Fraser, Trenholm, in this contract were cover for Confederate purchasers (to avoid capture). Greenwood and Batley were to ship machinery to Nassau. Fraser, Trenholm had already lost a ship to the*

U.S. navy, and it was thought that the latter might respect a native British manufacturer. Huse was called to give evidence in the case on September 25th, 1868.

2. Latin for out of luck (literally: royally screwed).
3. The Schooner *Stephen Hart* V. United States, Case No 126. Jan 11, 1866. Lawyers Co-op Publishing Company. In an interesting side note to the case, the text of the written opinion mistakenly refers to Saul as Paul Isaac.
4. Blatchford, Samuel. *Reports of Cases in Prize*. US District Court (New York) and US Circuit Court, published 1866. pp 427-466. Ibid, p. 444
5. Stowell, Ellory C., Munro, H.F. *International Cases Arbitrations and Incidents Illustrative of International Law, Volume II: War and Neutrality.* Houghton-Mifflin, 1916, p. 388.
6. In a US prize court case, the examination of witnesses is held before commissioners appointed by the prize court. The evidence is taken privately.
7. Ibid, Stowell, p. 391-395.
8. Ibid, Stowell, see also: Wallace: *Supreme Court Reports,* vol. v, p. 21.
9. Ibid, Stowell, see also: *Parliamentary Papers* [1900], *Miscellaneous,* No. 1, pp. 22-23.
10. Alderman, Geoffrey, *Modern British Jewry*, Oxford University Press, 1998, p. 63. See also: Caplan, M. *Tory's First Jewish MP* (March 1974) p. 9
11. The Jewish Chronicle, *10th June 1870, p10*
12. Ibid, *1st July 1870, p2*
13. Woodward, Henry, *The Geologist magazine*, CXV to CXXVI, Volume I, London: Trubner & Co, 1874, p. 315. Note: A colliery is a coalmine.
14. Lease from the Duke of Newcastle to Saul Isaac, Nottinghamshire Archives. NCB 3/5/1/3, 15th June 1875.
15. The archives record several lawsuits making it to the High Court over the years, always with Saul as the defendant, and a bank or other lender as plaintiff, but the outcome is not known. One can conclude two things from Saul's small estate at the end of his life: first that he continued his larcenous ways; and second that he lost most of those cases brought against him by his creditors.

CONCLUSION

The Isaacs were commercial opportunists with an objective to make as much profit as they could from the fraternal slaughter across the pond, by just about any means necessary. The timing of the US Civil War proved fortuitous as the firm desperately needed the business having lost their military contracts with the British army. And although the bookkeeping practices of S. Isaac, Campbell & Co were shady, the dichotomy was that the firm remained quite loyal to the Confederacy, even to the point of supplying their own blockade running fleet and advancing their own money when credit was necessary. There is some cock-eyed logic to the Isaacs' claim that the hidden commissions charged the Confederate Government were not unreasonable or excessive due to the poor state of Confederate credit. In addition, there were great risks involved for the firm such as the loss of two SIC & Co blockade runners to the Union. However, it is hard to get around the fact if a fair premium for risk was indeed the case, then the full extent of all charges should have been disclosed. The second set of books was damning, and there was no justifiable explanation for that.

Looking at the role of Caleb Huse, it is difficult to conclude that he was not either naïve or delusional for permitting a firm with the ill repute of SIC & Co to handle most of the CS Ordnance Department purchases without very close supervision. And while Huse's and SIC's defence was that splitting commissions was the English way of doing business in the 1860s, it was in no way, shape or form the right thing to do and everyone involved knew it. (1) If Huse was not ultimately found guilty of any malfeasance in his dealings with SIC & Co, it seems fairly clear that the Confederate Government did not intend for him to share commissions from the purchases brokered by the Isaacs' firm, and certainly not to use those funds for his own expenses or a War Department library. (2) And further, the CS Government did not agree to be overcharged for their purchases under any circumstances. In the final analysis, in 1861 the Ordnance Department needed military supplies fast, and in large quantities; SIC & Co stepped to fill that void and Huse went above the call of duty by purchasing goods for the Quartermaster's Department well before their own agents arrived, even though he had no obligation to do so. However, by mid-1863 one wonders if Huse had not received enough in commissions for that war library, and why he never mentioned his plans for that to Josiah Gorgas. (3)

Some good did, of course, come out of the McRae inquiry. It brought to light the helter-skelter purchasing by agents of various departments and commands which led to competition and resulted in higher prices for the government. In addition, McRae complained to Gorgas that the Confederacy was missing out completely by not taking blockade running into their own hands. He went as far as to say that, not a bale of cotton should be allowed to go out of the country nor a pound of merchandise go in, except on government account. (4) Gorgas for his part agreed, but only after the government had purchased additional vessels. The point is that additional attention was paid to the efficiency of not only the purchasing operation, and the Erlanger loan but also the shipping of goods through the blockade to Confederate ports. And with the improved supervision by the resolute Colin McRae, purchases took on the efficiency and organization of the rest of the Ordnance Department. The Isaacs, of course, would soon find themselves on the outside looking in, and desperate to get their enormous unpaid bill settled.

The quality of some of the goods brokered by SIC & Co for the Confederacy no doubt left something to be desired, including cloth of middling quality, and accoutrements made from less expensive cuts of leather with marginal craftsmanship. However, there is no arguing that early in the war, without the talent, energy, and determination of Caleb Huse, and the full financial and logistical backing of S. Isaac, Campbell & Co, the Confederacy had only limited means to maintain and equip their armies in the field. One is left wondering in the end, without Caleb Huse and S. Isaac, Campbell & Co, just how long might the newly formed Confederate States of America have expected to last, armed with antique muskets, shotguns, pikes and brickbats? (5) The question is a fair one, and might provide fuel for friendly discourse around the campfire with your messmates; talking history with knowledgeable friends and smoking a bowl of good Virginia Orinoco are still two of life's simple pleasures.

NOTES:

1. It was common for a firm to offer purchasing agents placing large orders a commission as a reward for their business. Indeed, Alexander Ross (Ross & Co) stated that it was an established rule to offer such inducements.
2. The War Department library excuse provided by Huse as a way of explaining the acceptance of substantial funds from the Isaacs is puzzling to this day. Of what use would a collection of military books be to the Confederacy, unless they could use them for cannon fodder? There is no evidence that Gorgas or Seddon tasked him with the job of procuring a library for the Confederate States, and permitting overcharges to do so. One wonders what Huse was thinking when he offered up that particular explanation.
3. Maybe he forgot to tell Gorgas or the matter never came up? Huse had received a small fortune from SIC & Co by mid-1863. It is impossible to know exactly how much, but reasonable estimates would be a few hundred thousand dollars in modern currency, and maybe a lot more. Huse had the benefit of writing his side of the story in 1904, after almost everyone involved was long gone.
4. The War of Rebellion, the Official Records of the Union and Confederate Armies, US Government Printing Office (1900), Series IV, Vol. II, p. 889-890. McRae writing to Gorgas from Paris on September, 4, 1863.
5. A brickbat is a piece of broken masonry often used as a weapon by mobs during a riot. The point being, the CS army needed modern military equipment to have any chance of winning their independence against a better equipped invading force.

The only known picture of Saul Isaac (front), outside his Colliery in Nottingham.
(*Courtesy Nottingham Central Library*)

APPENDIX A

British firms that conducted business with the Confederacy

British Firms that Conducted Business with the Confederacy

Aberdeen, Scotland
J&J Crombie & Co

Belfast, Northern Ireland
B. & E. McHugh

Birkenhead
Birkenhead Iron Works
Laird Brothers

Birmingham Small Arms Trade (BSAT)
Cooper & Goodman
Pryse & Redman
Joseph Wilson
Joseph Bourne
EC Hackett
Thomas Turner
WL Sargant & Son
Bentley & Playfair
Joseph Smith
King & Phillips
R & W Aston
Swinburn & Son

Charles Maybury
W Scott & Sons
Isaac Hollis & Sons
William Tranter
CW James
Robert Hughes
Ward & Son
E. Bond

Birmingham
Barner & Sons
Chatwin & Sons
WH Dowler
Firmin & Son
J. R. Grant & Son
S Buckley & Co
Smith & Wright Ltd
Smith, Kemp & Wright
WM Middlemore

Clydebank, Scotland
John Brown & Co

Dumbarton, Scotland
Denny Brothers

Glasgow, Scotland
Chamberlain & Co
Clyde Bank Foundry
Patrick Henderson & Co
James & George Thompson

Kelvinhaugh, Scotland
Alexander Stephen & Sons

Leeds
Greenwood & Batley Ltd

Liverpool
Ashbridge & Co
Blakely Ordnance Co
Gordon Coleman & Co
Collie, Westhead & Co
Curry, Killoch & Co
Cyclops Steel & Iron Works
Fawcett, Preston & Co
Fletcher, Hall & Stone
George Forrester & Co
Edward Lawrence & Co
Leech, Harrison & Forwood
Low Moor Iron Works
William C.Miller & Son
Old Tug Co
J. Stewart Oxley & Co

London
Alexander Ross & Co
Albion Trading Co
Alexander Collie & Co
Blakely Ordnance Co
Curtis & Harvey
Christy's Hatmakers
De La Rue & Co
Dudgeon Brothers
Emile Erlanger & Co
Galway Co
Graysbrook
John K. Gilliat & Co
Overed Guerney & Co
Hebbert & Co
T. & C. Hood
S. Isaac, Campbell & Co
Sinclair, Hamilton & Co
John Lane, Hankey & Co
W. S. Lindsay & Co
Zachariah C. Pearson & Co

Railway Carriage Makers Railway Works
RT Tait & Co
Robinson & Cottum
J. Henry Schroder & Co
S. Straker & Sons
William & Co
William Essex & Son
Charles William & Co
F. Wentworth & Co

London Commercial Gunmakers
Potts and Hunt
Parker Field & Sons
JE Barnett & Sons
EP Bond
Freed & Co
James Yeomans
London Armoury Co
Keen & Son
Wilkinson
Holland & Holland

Manchester
Hammond, Turner & Bates
Lomnitz & Co
Manchester Ordnance & Rifle Co
Joseph Whitworth & Co

Newcastle-Upon-Tyne
W. G. Armstrong & Co
Elswick Ordnance Works

Northampton
Turner Bros. Hyde & Co

Paisley, Scotland
J&P Coates

Sheffield
William Butcher Jr. & Co

Yorkshire (County)
Joshua Ellis & Sons

Source: Updated version of Lester, Richard I. Confederate Finance and Purchasing in Great Britain. Charlottesville: University of Virginia Press, 1975. Appendix IX

APPENDIX B

Partial text of report of the investigation of Weedon Depot

It devolved upon Mr. Elliott, on his arrival at Weedon, on the 7th December, 1855, to organize the establishment, taking the ordnance regulations as his basis, and to initiate a system of book-keeping. We are desirous to keep our account of the system of book-keeping adopted, as far as possible distinct from the narrative of the general mode in which the business was conducted; but it is, perhaps, hardly possible entirely to dissever the two subjects. To make either intelligible, it may be convenient to proceed, in the first instance, chronologically with the history of the establishment.

No books whatever had been kept previous to Mr. Elliott's arrival the only records of the stores previously received at the depot being the bills of delivery from the storekeeper's office at the Tower, Woolwich, and other military establishments, in respect of goods sent from those departments, and inspection notes, which accompanied the delivery of goods furnished by contractors. For the accounts which Mr. Elliott had to keep, and the correspondence he had to conduct, he was for the first five months after his arrival supplied with only five temporary clerks, "necessarily very young men, with no experience," all perfectly ignorant of the duties of an ordnance station, and only one of whom afterwards passed his examination. Mr. Elliott's own statement is, and we believe it to be true, that seeing the utter impossibility of establishing so large a system of book-keeping as he would have done with more ample means, the utmost he could do was to subdivide his duties into several branches: the saddlery branch, the boot branch, the cloth branch, and the garniture branch, and to direct the foreman in each of these branches to keep an account of the daily receipts and issues. He then "started a ledger as well as he could, in the roughest possible way, and set a clerk to work upon it."The number of clerks was gradually increased. In July, 1856, there were eight clerks. In November, 1856, they consisted of eleven; and in March, 1857, in consequence of Mr. Elliott's urgent representation of the necessity of further clerical assistance, three additional temporary clerks were added. These, fourteen in all, constituted the book-keeping establishment until September, 1857 a number wholly inadequate to the rapidly increasing duties which they had to perform.

Besides the rapid despatch of troops to China and India in the spring and summer of 1857, nearly 50,000 men were added to the army between January, 1857, and May, 1858, and 30,000 embodied militia were called out in the course of the same year, 1857. This last measure alone doubled in one week the work at Weedon. On the 1st of September, 1857, four clerks were added to the office, and shortly afterwards, Mr. Tatum, an experienced military storekeeper, with an assistant, Mr. Munro, were added to Mr. Elliott's staff. By this time, considerable arrears existed in the books, and upon a representation of Mr. Tatum, strongly backed by Mr. Elliott, of the necessity for further assistance, both in the store and book-keeping department, six clerks and four persons intended to act as storeholders were sent down in October, but none of the latter being conversant with the issue or management of stores, Mr. Elliott appropriated all ten to the book-keeping department, the duties of which were largely increasing.

According to the Ordnance regulations, the store ledger of every station is made up to the 31st March in each year, and should be ready for transmission to the War Office within four months after the expiration of the financial year. It was not considered necessary that Mr. Elliott should transmit the ledger made up to the 31st March, 1856, when he had been less than four months at Weedon. His first ledger, therefore, comprised a period of sixteen months ending on the 31st March, 1857, and would have been due at the War Office not later than the 1st of August, 1857. It did not arrive, although he sent up according to regulation a balance sheet purporting to show the amount of stores received, issued, and remaining in hand at the station, and which should have been compiled from the store ledger. He was called upon for explanation as to this balance sheet, and directed to send up the store ledger itself. But he is stated to have "fenced" with this demand, in other words, he urged as an excuse for its non-production, "the deficient clerical assistance" at his command. In August, 1857, it was resolved that Mr. Elliott should be transferred to the post of storekeeper at Dublin, and be succeeded at Weedon by Captain Gordon. This change was not resolved on from any suspicion as to Mr. Elliott's honesty; but it was thought that on account of Captain Gordon's military experience, he would carry on the duties in a more satisfactory manner than Mr. Elliott. The change could not, however, conveniently take place until after the Dublin storekeeper had made his annual demand. Mr. Elliott appears to have continued to make frequent representations of the arrears in his books, and the impossibility of overcoming them when the whole time of the clerks was occupied with the current work of the office; and at length, in February, 1858, partly in consequence of these representations and partly from the opinion expressed by Captain Gordon of the necessity of changes in the mode of conducting the business at Weedon, Major Marvin was sent down to investigate "the past and present state of the establishment," and, among other things, to inquire into the state of the ledger. Just before Major Marvin went down, ten additional clerks were appointed and sent down to Weedon, making the total number thirty-seven. But we have been informed by Captain Gordon that, instead of an increase of ten clerks, there should have been an increase of twenty-three: that was the lowest number he agreed with an experienced officer in the War Department in considering necessary; and in February, 1858, they made a joint representation to this effect to Captain Caffin, the director of clothing.

Captain Gordon succeeded Mr. Elliott as storekeeper on the 14th of May, 1858, when the "remain" or stocktaking of the stores at Weedon was completed, and they were formally handed over to him by Mr. Elliott. **The ledger of 1856-7, however, was not quite completed, when, on the 22nd of May, 1858, Mr. Elliott absconded, leaving England for America, abandoning his wife, and having an actress as the companion of his flight.** The ledger, on its completion early in June, 1858, was sent up to the War Office, and after a thorough examination (occupying nearly two months) with the vouchers 5,400 very few of which were missing, it appeared to be perfectly satisfactory, and complete as regards the issues or credit side of the account, while the receipts or debit side of the account only required verification by comparing them with the accounts of payments made for stores delivered at Weedon. This comparison and verification has since been satisfactorily completed. Whether the stores, which according to these accounts had been delivered at Weedon, were actually received there, could, however, only be ascertained accurately when the ledger of 1857-8 up to May 14th, 1858, had been completed, and the amounts then appearing in the ledger to the debit of the storekeeper had been compared with the actual stores handed over on that day to Captain Gordon on the completion of the remain. In order to prepare this second ledger, Commissary-General Adams, with a staff of eight officers, proceeded to Weedon, but, as they were not conversant with the system of accounts introduced by Mr. Elliott, the Commissioners engaged for the purpose the services of Mr. Jay, now of the firm of Messrs. Quilter, Ball and Jay, most experienced accountants in the city of London. We requested him, in the first instance, to examine the books kept at Weedon during Mr. Elliott's superintendence, and also those at present in use, with a view of ascertaining the respective merits and defects of the two systems. Messrs. Quilter and Co. have examined the books in use at Weedon since December, 1855 (upwards of 300 in number), and have made their report of the system upon which they have been kept.

It appears from that report that the bookkeeping at Weedon between December, 1855, and August, 1856, was of a very rough and imperfect description, and that there was no regular classification of the facts indicated by the original vouchers. The books then kept referred—1. To the registration of papers and correspondence (these are not strictly speaking books of account); 2. To dealings with contractors and tradesmen in connection with the receipt of stores; 3. To receipts of stores from Woolwich, the Tower, and other government stations ; 4. To orders for issues to regiments, and issues made accordingly. The accountants add, "Besides the books described above, a rough document was framed having the character of a store ledger, that is, containing accounts opened for some of the different descriptions of stores, with entries purporting to show the respective receipts and issues under distinctive heads, but it was never duly entered up, and as a book of results is perfectly useless. In addition to the foregoing, certain other books were kept by the inspectors and viewers in their respective store rooms; there was also a foreman's book of issues, and one for special issues of cloth, both of which were likewise kept in the store rooms.
"We see no reason to doubt that the entries made in these books were intended truthfully to record, and did in the main accurately record, the amount of stores received and inspected, packed, and issued in each branch of the depot. But our accountants are of opinion that "although these books existed

and entries more or less continuous were made in them, not one was kept efficiently and completely, and there was, properly speaking, no systematic book keeping; the consequence being a state of arrears and confusion which in a greater or less degree continued to characterize the accounts of the department down to the time when Captain Gordon took charge of it in May, 1858, and notwithstanding the improvements which Mr. Elliott himself introduced in August, 1856."

From and after the 22nd August, 1856, a more regular system of accounts was adopted which continued in operation during the remainder of Mr. Elliott's superintendence. The business of the depot was divided into four branches:—1. The registry branch, including all correspondence, letters both inward and outward, and the registration of papers and documents generally. 2. The contract branch, comprising the whole course of dealing with contractors and tradesmen in respect of supplies furnished by them, from the receipt of the goods at the depot to the granting of the certificates on which payment was made. 3. Receipt and issue branch. The business under this head consisted of taking account of articles brought into store, other than those received from contractors and tradesmen, and of all issues out of store. 4. Store ledger branch. The business of this branch was to collect in one record, viz., "the store ledger" on the one hand, all receipts of clothing and stores from every source, and on the other all issues of clothing and stores, with the view of exhibiting in debtor and creditor form under the head of each article, as "boots," "caps," "tunics," " trousers," &c., the periodical receipts and issues, and the balance or stock remaining on hand from time to time.

After a searching and laborious investigation into the accounts, during which the whole of the issues for the entire period from December, 1855, to May, 1858, have been traced to their various destinations, as indicated in the accounts, the accountants reported "that all stores delivered to Weedon, or coming within the scope of its official responsibility, have been substantially accounted for." And that "with respect to the personal accounts with contractors, they were enabled, after careful examination, to report that, excepting in some few and trifling instances, not calling for special observation, they found them to be essentially correct, and that no other moneys have been paid to the contractors than such as they became entitled to receive in consideration of stores delivered." And, finally, "that nothing came before them in the course of their investigation to warrant the suggestion of fraudulent practices by the late principal military storekeeper in dealing with the stores confided to his administration."

In the opinion thus expressed the Commissioners entirely concurred; and they continued: We have great satisfaction in expressing to your Majesty our belief, that whatever suspicions may have been naturally excited, there has been, as regards the stores at Weedon, no dishonest dealing whatever. Everything which has been paid for has been received, and no defalcation has taken place. To have arrived at this conclusion makes us regret less than we should otherwise regret the time, labour, and money spent in this inquiry. Nothing, indeed, can be a greater proof of the confusion and arrears into which the store accounts had fallen than the fact that it has taken Messrs. Quilter, Ball and Jay eight months at least to complete the ledgers, and to arrive at the judgment on them above expressed.

As regards the cash accounts of Mr. Elliott, they were entirely distinct from, and unconnected with, the store accounts. All payments for supplies delivered at Weedon were made by drafts upon the paymaster-general, no storekeeper being allowed to have anything to do with the money transactions relating to the supply of stores. But it was Mr. Elliott's duty as storekeeper to pay the weekly wages of the foremen and labourers employed at the depot. These payments were always duly made by him, and entered in check and pay lists, as laid down in the ordnance regulations. He was also entrusted with the duty of paying the charges of carriers for goods delivered at Weedon. For these purposes he made monthly, as is the custom with all storekeepers, a demand for the sum necessary for the expenses of the following month. Each demand showed the amount remaining to his debit after payment of the expenses of the preceding month. These demands during 1857 were for about 1,000L a month. His cash accounts, with the necessary vouchers to support them, were sent in quarterly, in accordance with the regulations, fourteen days after the expiration of the quarter. His quarterly account ending 31st December, 1857, was rendered accordingly, showing a small balance against him. His monthly demands for January, February, March, and April, 1858, including a demand of more than 1,600L for carriage of stores, were granted. But as he neglected to send in his quarterly account up to the 31st March, 1858, within the fourteen days prescribed, he was peremptorily called on to do so, and in default of his furnishing it, the accountant general refused the imprest for 2,000L demanded by him for the month of May. Had the quarterly account ending March, 1858, been sent in, it must have been at once discovered that carriers' bills for 1,639L., in respect of which he had obtained imprests, had not been paid by him. Mr. Elliott had also previously received instructions to make up his cash account to the date of his leaving Weedon for the post of store-keeper at Dublin, to hand over the balance in his hands to his successor, Captain Gordon, and to produce his receipt for the balance.

On the 15th May Mr. Elliott borrowed the sum of *500L* from a contractor, out of which he paid *250L* for the weekly wages of the establishment, which he appears never to have allowed to fall into arrear. Shortly after his disappearance on the 22nd of May, it was discovered that bills for the carriage of stores, amounting to 1,639L.13s.4d. were unpaid by him, and that (including this sum) the balance due to the public from him was 2,048L. 10s. *6d.* In accordance with the provisions of the Statute 52 Geo. III. c. 66, and the Ordnance Regulation No. 99, Mr. Elliott, on entering on his office at Weedon, gave security in a bond for *2,000L.*, entered into by a guarantee association on his behalf for the due performance of his duties. This *2,000L* has since been paid by the guarantee association, so that the actual loss in cash occasioned by Mr. Elliott's deficiencies is reduced to 48L. 10s. *6d.* His cash accounts appear to have been kept with entire accuracy, and by the proper system of double entry.

Upon a review of the whole evidence the commissioners expressed their opinion that the general mode in which the business of the Weedon establishment was conducted was far from satisfactory.

We have specified, perhaps in tedious detail, the main defects and irregularities which existed there. The principal blame which we can attach to Mr. Elliott, apart from the admitted deficiency in his cash balance, is in respect of his frequent absences from Weedon. No doubt it was often necessary for him to attend at the War Office and Mark Lane. But there is too much reason to believe that much of the time during which he was absent was devoted to his private pleasures in neglect of his public duty. When at his post he seems to have worked diligently. We acquit him of any deliberate intention to do wrong either in his so-called deviations from the ordnance system of accounts, or in not keeping distinct the inspection and custody of the stores. We think that he was not sufficiently peremptory in insisting upon having the further help which he required. In our opinion the main defects in the

Weedon establishment are chargeable to the War Department. 1. It was a mistake to fix the clothing depot so far from London, beyond the opportunity of immediate and frequent personal surveillance by the director and assistant director of clothing, and separated from the important branch establishment in Mark Lane. This mistake has now been remedied by the abandonment of Weedon as a depot for clothing, and the removal of the establishment to Pimlico. 2. It was a mistake to appoint the first head of the establishment without specific instructions as to its organization. 3. It was a great mistake to supply him at the outset of the undertaking with a small and inexperienced staff. The inspection staff in particular ought to have been organized from the commencement upon the plan adopted at the Tower, and better salaries should have been given to the various inspectors. 4. It was a continuing mistake not to increase the staff in proportion to the increase of the work in accordance with Mr. Elliott's frequently repeated requests. 5. It was a mistake, notwithstanding the distance of Weedon from London, that more frequent visits were not paid there by the directors of clothing, and a more rigid supervision exercised over the books and the stores. 6. It was a mistake not to have had a more considerable store in hand before commencing the issues, so as to have been prepared for the emergencies which arose. 7. It was, we think, a most serious mistake to have separate contracts for the cloth required, and for the making that cloth into garments; a course involving double contracts, double correspondence, double inspection, double carriage, double keeping of accounts. This defect has been cured, the contracts being now in the first instance entered into for the clothing completely made up.

These defects, together with the absence of proper patterns, the discrepancies between patterns and specifications, the haste with which tenders were called for, the delay in informing the storekeeper of the contracts entered into, the delivery of kits at Weedon, all these have satisfied us that the new system of clothing the army, however advantageous in many respects, was inaugurated without due consideration, and certainly without adequate provision for so extensive a change. Neither the arrangements made nor the agents employed in making them were sufficient for the vast amount of labour which the new system required. The laudable object of the War Department doubtless was to add the recommendation of economy to those to which their new system might be otherwise entitled. With this view the establishment was stinted and the inspectors were miserably underpaid. Officers of intelligence, ability, and practical experience received salaries of only 100L. a year, a sum quite insufficient for the decent support of themselves and of their families. Yet to them was entrusted the power to decide upon the acceptance or rejection of goods of very large value, which contractors naturally wished not to have returned upon their hands. The result was inevitable. These officers were thereby subjected not only to the suspicion that their services were considered of little value by their superiors, but to the graver imputation that persons so inadequately remunerated might be ready to show favour from corrupt motives to any contractor who could purchase their good will. We think there is no ground for such imputations. We acquit not only Mr. Elliott, but all the officers of the War Department, as well as the inspectors and subordinate officers at Weedon, of having shown partiality or favour towards any contractor and we have much pleasure in adding that a suggestion made before the Committee of the House of Commons on Contracts implying that favouritism had been shown to a particular contractor in respect of cloth delivered at Weedon was frankly withdrawn before us by the witness who had made it. We think there was ground for some suspicion in the first instance, but the explanation given of the facts cleared up the points, removed the impression on the mind of the witness himself, and entirely satisfied us that no undue preference had been shown.

Source: Annals of British Legislation :
Being a Classified and Analysed Summary of Public Bills, Statutes, Accounts and Papers, p 110-117.

APPENDIX C

Elliott letter

ELLIOTT LETTER

Extract from: The Royal Commission of Army Contracts.
The Times Newspaper, November 1858.

The letter from James Elliott to Samuel Isaac which was read out to the Commission.

New York August 30th

"Dear Sir – Having read in the papers a statement referring to the loan of £500 made by you to me, and to various public dealings with you as a contractor, which statement, if explained, might give to these transactions character not in accordance with the facts, I think it right, both in justice to myself and to you, to say that, as to the £500 having been given as a bribe, or for any favours shown to you in the discharge of my public duties, the assertion is a cowardly and calamitous falsehood, which no man, however high his position, would dare to advance were I in England. The certificates for stores not delivered must, to any man conversant with the practice of the service, be an obvious impossibility. The certificate, previous to receiving my signature must of necessity have received those of the inspectors who examined the stores both as to quantity and quality, and upon the faith of those signatures would have been attached, and without those, notwithstanding my signature, the Accountant- General would not allow the claim for payment.

"In no way and on no occasion have I favoured or offered facilities to your firm which were not extended equally to all other contractors, among these are many men of high honour and character; to them I may confidently appeal as to whether I have not on all occasions endeavoured to the utmost of the meagre assistance sparingly afforded to me, to ensure them promptitude of payment and a fair inspection of their supplies.

"That I ever allowed you or any other contractor to suffer by my neglect of duty or absence from Weedon, I utterly and emphatically deny. No man ever made himself more a slave to the public service than I did. Had I been less zealous I might have been less maligned by those who deem it honourable to cover their own defects at the expense of an absent and oppressed man who, had descended to what they would attribute to him during the past twenty years of his serfdom, possessed ample opportunity for becoming as wealthy and adulated as to be now poor and unfriended.

"I regret my inability at present to repay you the £500 but shall esteem it and first lieu upon whatever balance is due to me from the government arising out of a claim which I am now prosecuting exceeding the amount against me by the War Department, and which however at present opposed, I believe to be irresistible both in law and equity.

"I may add that I am ready at any moment to declare, on oath, that the loan of £500 was the first and only private monetary transaction of any description between us, which, at the time of borrowing, I was fully persuaded it would have been in my power to replace out of money that I then had a prospect of raising.

I remain dear Sir yours truly,

W Elliott"

APPENDIX D

Alexander Collie & Co

ALEXANDER COLLIE & COMPANY

The heroes and villains of history often occupy the gray areas around the fringes of good and evil. In a story like this one, full of marginal scoundrels, once in a while history provides us with a schemer whose character seems a notch below all the others. One such person was Alexander Collie, a charlatan even by the standards of some of the men masquerading as respectable in the financial houses of Victorian London, like SIC & Co.

As discussed elsewhere in this monograph, William Crenshaw who, along with Major James Ferguson, might rightly be distinguished as the villains of the SIC & Co/Caleb Huse tale, came to London in early 1863 with a scheme to profit from running supplies past the Union blockade. Crenshaw was a private businessman from Richmond, and not a member or a representative of the Confederate Government, though his mission had their support. And as fate would have it, he promptly found his way to the firm of Alexander Collie & Co of Manchester. (1)

Alexander Collie was born in Aberdeen, Scotland in 1823, the son of a merchant. He started business in Manchester in about 1850 and by 1863 had established a warehouse in London. His business was the import and export of cotton in its various forms. His brother William joined him in the venture, running the Manchester part of the business, while Alexander concentrated on the London side of the enterprise. George Collie (Liverpool) was another brother and is not to be confused with the separate businesses of Alexander and William. (2)

Crenshaw pitched the idea of a joint venture with Collie for the creation of a private steamship line, of which half the cargo would be for the CS War Department. In other words, this venture would amount to a virtual monopoly on all Quartermaster and Commissary supplies run through the blockade and a commission on the goods either way, captured or not. Structured as such, it would be difficult to miss the deal, and smelling money, Alexander Collie agreed. He advanced the money for the first steamship *Havana*. The initial appeal to investors was based on the assumption, which proved false, that the Union blockade would not disturb commercial vessels filled with Quartermaster and Commissary goods, which could be classified as non-contraband under international law. In contrast, Ordnance Department supplies were (of course) always classified as contraband and thus subject to seizure as a prize of war. (3) The Union proved not as cooperative as hoped, and did not abide by that minor distinction. Colin McRae had a lack of enthusiasm for the Crenshaw/Collie venture from the start, seeing problems where greedier people saw financial gain. As things developed, Crenshaw and Collie had joint interests in some steam ships and not in others. Collie, for instance, had a side deal going on with the state of North Carolina for proprietary supplies backed by their own cotton, which did not involve supplies for the Government in Richmond. Since states rights was a key provision of the reason behind secession from the Union, state-owned vessels were exempt from the general requirement that half the cargo space on merchant vessels be reserved for the CS Government.

An odd and interesting series of tragedies began to befall Crenshaw and then subsequently, his vessels. First, in mid-May 1863 his Richmond factory burned to the ground, leaving only his steamship enterprise as a source of income. Then over a short period, the Crenshaw steamships began to suffer a disproportionate number of captures compared to those being operated separately by A. Collie & Co. To wit, Crenshaw lost seven steamships in the summer of 1864, all on either their first or second voyage, while Collie & Co enjoyed a much more successful record, including those shipments for the old North state (NC). The *Richmond Examiner* wondered aloud (in mid August 1864) if Collie might be intentionally endangering the ships of a rival line, and questioning the motives of their agent in Wilmington, NC, identified as a Hebrew. (4) Collie shot back a vitriolic response, which oddly failed to address the charges made by the Richmond newspaper.

This much is known, the port of Wilmington, NC was at the time (arguably) the second most important city in the Confederacy after Richmond. Wilmington was running almost three times the volume of cargo of Charleston. However, it was also becoming a notoriously mean place as a result. One officer recalled shortly after the Civil War,

"Talk about Yankees worshipping the almighty dollar! You should have seen the adoration paid the Golden Calf at Wilmington during the days of blockade-running."

Alexander Collie & Co had a staff of agents from England handling their business interests in Wilmington. The situation was described as follows:

"Wilmington during that period swarmed with foreigners, Jews and Gentiles. In fact, going down the main street or along the river, you might well imagine you were journeying from Jerusalem to Jericho. As to the falling among thieves we will make no mention... At every turn you "met up," as our tarheel friends say, with young Englishmen dressed like grooms and jockeys, or with a peculiar coachman-like look, seeming, in a foreign land, away from their mothers, to indulge their fancy for the outré and extravagant in dress to the utmost. These youngsters had money, made money, lived like fighting-cocks, and astonished the natives by their pranks, and the way they flung the Confederate "stuff" about. Of course they were deeply interested in the Confederate cause, and at the same time wanted cotton. The Manchester house of Alexander Collie and Co. had quite a regiment of these youngsters in their employ. Fine-looking fellows, with turned-up noses, blue eyes wide apart, and their fluffy, straw colored, mutton-chop whiskers floating in the wind, to the great admiration of their chèr amiés, the handsome quadroon washer-women, on whose mantle-pieces and in whose albums were frequently to be found photographs strikingly resembling the aforesaid young foreigners. They occupied a large flaring yellow house, like a military hospital, at the upper end of Market Street, and which belonged to a Mr. Wright. There these youngsters kept open house and spent their Company's money, while it lasted. There they fought cocks on Sundays, until the neighbours remonstrated and threatened prosecution..." (5)

Lest you feel sorry for the author's caricature of the British lads working for Alexander Collie & Co, he continues to say of another disliked contingent,

"The tribe of Benjamin was also very well represented at Wilmington, as you may imagine, the unctuous and oleaginous Confederate Secretary of State having well provided for "his people." A great many gentle-men of strongly Jewish physiognomy were to be met with on the streets, in very delicate health, and with papers in their pockets to keep them out of the army from the Secretary of State, but still in hot pursuit of the "monish." When the conscript officer became very zealous and pressing they fled away to Nassau and Bermuda." (6)

Whatever the case, the fact remains that Collie's vessels were profitable while the vessels owned by Crenshaw lost the Quartermaster's Department not only substantial sums of money, but more importantly huge stores of provisions much needed to feed and clothe the Confederate armies in the field. Oddly enough, the Ordnance Department vessels did not suffer the same fate as the Quartermaster's (Crenshaw/Ferguson) in running the blockade, as they were not carrying supplies in competition with A. Collie, or perhaps they were just luckier. Those doing business with A. Collie & Co seldom met with good fortune. Peter Tait of Limerick partnered with Collie for his woollen material in filling his contract for Confederate uniforms. And further, to supply the Confederacy from Britain or Ireland entailed running the Union blockade. Toward this end, Tait again came into contact with Alexander Collie & Co, owner or part owner of several infamous blockade runners. One recent author quite adamantly contends that Collie & Co. repeatedly cheated Tait by hiding the accounts of profits or sales from him. Whether true or not, at the end of war, Collie & Co presented Tait with a bill for approximately £30,000, his share of their venture's losses, and Peter Tait had never lost a single shipment to the Union blockade.

In an odd twist of fate or perhaps karmic retribution, all of the duplicitous dealing on the part of Alexander Collie & Co came home to roost about ten years post-bellum in 1875. Collie & Co never quite recovered from the collapse of the Confederacy and the loss of the cotton to confiscation and sale by the Union Treasury Department. (7) The following account summarizes a huge scandal that made the bookkeeping exploits of the Isaacs seem trivial and amateurish by comparison, as in fact, they were:

"In the middle of June, 1875, disaster again occurred this time in the Manchester and India trade by the failure of Alexander Collie & Co., of

Manchester and Leadenhall Street, London, and in consequence this year became known then, and since, as the "Collie" year. The liabilities of this Firm were estimated at three millions; but Firm after Firm, as a result of the failure of this house, suspended payment, one house having nominal liabilities of two and a-half millions.

The firm of Collie & Co consisted of two brothers, Alexander and William Collie. The trustee in bankruptcy was the late Mr. John Young, of Turquand, Young, and the realisation of the Estate proved to be a lingering and disastrous one for the Creditors, the actual amount of dividend paid by this particular estate being disbursed in six instalments, in 1876, 1878, 1880, 1883, 1885, and the final closing of account took place in June, 1889. At meetings of Creditors, and by statements from responsible quarters, it transpired that the debtors had been living in all the prodigality of luxury that between them they had been in the habit of drawing 20,000 a year for their personal expenditure, Mr. Alexander Collie having drawn 123,000 for himself. The lease of Alexander Collie's house in Kensington Palace Gardens sold for 38,500, and the "costly contents" were the subject of five days' sale. (8) It is notorious in connection with that year, that, as a consequence of losses sustained, the leading Joint Stock Banks had to reduce their half-yearly Dividends, in addition to otherwise providing for the losses sustained.

A feature of this Firm's transactions was, that they did not accept Bills, and there was not a single acceptance of theirs existent at the date of their failure. They drew upon Houses many of whom were entirely of their own creation, and who were financed by them. On the 2ist July both Partners, whose capital existed only in name, were charged at the Guildhall Police Court for having obtained money by false pretences, in drawing Bills with marks and numbers upon them, indicating that they referred to Cotton and Ledger accounts; but in fact, they were only Accommodation Bills. (9) It was proved that there were no such goods sold, no such accounts in the ledger, and no goods accounts between the acceptors and the guarantors. As a matter of fact, goods to the extent of 100,000 roughly, were all that were represented in millions of Bills in the hands of Banks and other Firms. On the 8th August it was announced that Alexander Collie had absconded. Warrants were granted for his apprehension, but he was not arrested, and it was afterwards ascertained that he was in Spain, between which country and this at that time, no extradition treaty existed. The charge was not proceeded with as against William Collie, and Alexander Collie died in

New York on 23rd November, 1895...The effect of this failure was severely felt in the Manchester and India Goods markets." (10)

It is difficult to sympathize with the fate of the larcenous British expatriate Alexander Collie, except to the extent that he may have served as an antagonist to the *Agents Provocateurs* Crenshaw and Ferguson.

NOTES:

1. The *Richmond Examiner* able to size up Mr. Collie quickly enough, referring to him in an April 1864 article as a *pawky* Scotchman. *Pawky* being a period term for cunning or shrewd, but not in a complimentary sense.
2. Waite, John E, *Peter Tait: A Remarkable Story*, Milnford Publications 2005. p. 49.
3. Wilson, Harold, *Confederate Industry: Manufacturers and Quartermasters in the Civil War*, University of Mississippi Press, 2002, p. 172.
4. Ibid, Wilson, p. 173, excerpt from the *Richmond Examiner*, reprinted in the *New York Times* on August 21, 1864.
5. Johns, J. *Wilmington, NC during the Blockade, by a Late Confederate Officer,* Harpers New Monthly Magazine, September 1866.
6. Ibid, Johns. The author considers Scotchmen about on par with the Jews in terms of business acumen noting the Wilmington area was settled by, "*Scotchmen, and to this day you find the old Highland names, and see strongly marked Scottish features among the inhabitants. The people still retain many of the traits of their descent, and are shrewd, canny, money-making, and not to be beaten at driving a bargain by any Yankee that we ever saw."*
7. See *Young v United States*, 97 US 39, (1877). Trustees for the Creditors from the Bankruptcy of Collie & Co brought suit to recover cotton the firm claimed as their sole possession, and unsuccessfully made their claim under the Abandoned and Captured Property Act.
8. Including his extensive collection of artwork, such as the famous Victorian painting by John Millais, called *Hearts are Trump*. Kensington was where Samuel Isaac lived, too, in a nearby estate liquidated a few years earlier.
9. Accommodation Bills are bills of exchange, signed by a guarantor, who pays in the place of the acceptor should he default at maturity. This is also known as kiting and it means commercial paper (supposedly secured by

commodities, in this case non-existent) is moved from Bank to Bank one deposit covering the withdrawal from the previous institution. A Banker named Benson suffered in this scam, and opined that if British Banks were not so notoriously secretive and private, Collie could not have gotten by his shenanigans for as long as he did.

10. Woolley, Charles, *Phases of Panic: A Brief Historical Review*, Henry Good & Son Publisher, 1896, p. 37-38.

APPENDIX E

HUSE'S BRITISH IMPORTS

By the end of 1862, the amount of military goods imported from Great Britain was huge as this following letter written by Gorgas on February 3rd 1863, to Confederate Secretary of War James ASeddon, indicates.

ABSTRACT OF SUMMARY STATEMENT SHOWING QUANTITY AND VALUE OF ARMY SUPPLIES PURCHASES AND SHIPPED BY MAJ C HUSE ON ACCOUNT OF CONFEDERATE STATES GOVERNMENT.

131,129 Stands of Arms as follows: 70,980 long Enfield Rifles, 9,715 short Enfield rifles, 354 carbine Enfield rifles, 27,000 Austrian rifles, 21,040 British muskets, 20 small bore Enfield, 2,020 Brunswick rifles, at a cost including cases, molds, kegs, screw drivers & c of £417,263,9s 11d

129 cannon as follows: 54 6 pounder bronze guns, smooth; 18 howitzer bronze guns, smooth; 6 12 pounder iron guns, rifled; 2 howitzers, iron; carriages and caissons for same; 6 rifled Blakely cannon; 6 3. 10 inch carriages for same; 18,000 shells for same; 2,000 fuses; 3 rifled cannon, 8 inch Blakely; 680 shells for same; 12 rifled steel guns, 12 pounders; shot, shell & c, for same; 2 bronze guns, rifled, 200 shells and fuses; 756 shrapnel shell, round; 9,820 wooden fuses; 4 steel cannon, rifled, 9 pounders; 1,008 shells and fuses for same; 220 sets harness; spare parts artillery harness & c; all costing £96, 746 1s 8d
1,226 cavalry equipments, 16,178 cavalry sabers, 5,392 saber belts,5392 saber knots 1,360 cavalry humnals (sic) 1,386 cavalry surcingles and pads, total expended for cavalry £20,321 12s 3d
Fifty four sets web harness, 456 leather butts, 198 leather packages all costing £9,717,11s

34,731 Sets of accoutrements, 34,655 knapsacks complete, (Inc mess tins and covers) 81,406 bayonet scabbards, 4000 canteen straps, 40,240 gun slings, and 650 sergeants accoutrements all costing £54,873 16s 3d

357,000 pounds cannon powder 91,600 pounds musket powder, 94,600 pounds musket powder, 32,000 pounds rifle powder, 900 pounds bursting powder, 4,137,000 cartridges for small arms, 2,800 chlorate potassa (pounds) 1,024 hundred weight saltpetre, 89,900 friction tubes, 10,100,000 percussion caps, all costing £47,010 10s 3d

Quartermaster's Dept:

74,006 pairs of boots, costing £28,422 16s 4d, 62,025 blankets, £23,903 2s 11d 8, 250 pairs of trousers £5,144 11s 3d 170, 724 pairs of socks £9, 292 18s 7d, 78,520 yards of cloth £24,660 15s 5d 6,703 shirts £738 9s 8d and 8,375 greatcoats £13,294 17s 8d, 17,894 yards flannel £1,632 5d, 97 packages trimmings, £3,435 11s 6d total expended in clothing & c £110525 3s 9d

46 sets armourers tools, 36 sets saddlers tools, 10 sets furriers tools, 3,336 pieces serge for cartridge bags, 2,000 cartridge bags, 1,013 hundredweight lead, 100 hundredweight sheet copper, 16 flags, £13,482 10s 7d worth of medical supplies, 87 tarpaulins, 10 hundredweight shellac, 1,192 boxes tin plate, 75 packages steel, 64 hundredweight steel; total for medical supplies and other supplies as above £33,049 6s freight, railway carriage & c £49,683 19s 5d

Supplies that have been shipped	£	s	d
Small arms	417,262	9	11
Artillery and harness	96,746	1	8
Accoutrements & c	54,973	10	3
Ammunition	47,010	1	3
Leather	9,717	11	0
Clothing	110,525	3	9
Medical supplies	13,432	10	7
Ordnance stores	19,616	15	5
Freight, Railway carriage & c	19,732	7	9
Insurance & c	29,951	11	9
Total	£818,869	18	3

Supplies in London ready for shipment

	£	s	d
23,000 rifles to be delivered at Nassau	87,950	0	0
20,000 scabbards	1,500	0	0
46 casks saddlers material	631	5	0
11 nitric acid	38	4	8
2,012,000 cartridges	5,533	5	0
3,000,000 percussion caps	681	0	0
10,000 pouch tins for accoutrements	250	0	0
286 ingots tin	628	2	6
931 pigs lead	1,252	17	9
3 cases thread & c	240	17	3
1 bale serge	60	19	6
13,750 pairs trousers, QM dept	8,565	2	1
14,250 greatcoats QM dept	23,835	13	17
1,804 pair boots QM dept	887	11	6
4 chests tea, medical dept	48	7	6
Total	£249,853	1	0
Shipped up to date	£818,869	18	3

FEBRUARY 3, 1863

Respectfully referred to the Secretary of War for information as to purchases made by Major Huse

J GORGAS
Colonel, Chief of Ordnance

(OR Series IV Volume II, p 382-384)

APPENDIX F

The Springbok

U.S. Supreme Court

The Springbok, 72 U.S. 5 Wall. 1 1 (1866)
The Springbok
72 U.S. (5 Wall.) 1
Syllabus

1. Though invocation, in prize cases, is not regularly made on original hearing, but only after a cause has been fully heard on the ship's documents and the preparatory proofs, and where suspicious circumstances appear from these, yet where the court below, in the exercise of its discretion, has allowed it on first hearing, the decree will not necessarily be reversed, decrees of condemnation having passed in both the cases invoked, one *pro confesso* and the other by a decree of the highest appellate court.

2. Where the papers of a ship sailing under a charter party are all genuine and regular and show a voyage between ports neutral within the meaning of international law, where there has been no concealment nor spoliation of them, where the stipulations of the charter party in favor of the owners are apparently in good faith, where the owners are neutrals, have no interest in the cargo, and have not previously in any way violated neutral obligations, and there is no sufficient proof that they have any knowledge of the unlawful destination of the cargo, in such a case, its aspect being otherwise fair, the vessel will not be condemned because the neutral port to which it is sailing has been constantly and notoriously used as a port of call and trans shipment by persons engaged in systematic violation of blockade and in the

conveyance of contraband of war, and was meant by the owners of the cargo carried on this ship to be so used in regard to it.

3. The facts that the master declared himself ignorant as to what a part of his cargo, of which invoices were not on board (having been sent by mail to the port of destination) consisted, such part having been contraband, and also declared himself ignorant of the cause of capture, when his mate, boatswain and steward all testified that they understood it to be the vessel's having contraband on board, *held* not sufficient, of themselves, to infer guilt to the owners of the vessel, in no way compromised with the cargo. But the misrepresentation of the master as to his knowledge of the ground of capture *held* to deprive the owners of costs on restoration.

4. A cargo was here condemned for intent to run a blockade where the vessel was sailing to a port such as that above described, the bills of lading disclosing the contents of 619 packages of 2007 which made the cargo, the contents of the remaining 1388 being not disclosed; where both they and the manifest made the cargo deliverable to order, the master being directed by his letter of instructions to report himself on arrival at the neutral port to H., who "would give him orders as to the delivery of his cargo;" where a certain fraction of the cargo whose contents were undisclosed was specially fitted for the enemy's military use and a larger part capable of being adapted to it; where other vessels owned by the owners of the cargo, and by the charterer, and sailing ostensibly for neutral ports were, on invocation, shown to have been engaged in blockade running, many packages on one of the vessels, and numbered in a broken series of numbers, finding many of the complemental numbers on the vessel now under adjudication; where no application was made to take further proof in explanation of these facts, and the claim of the cargo, libeled at New York, was not personally sworn to by either of the persons owning it, resident in England, but was sworn to by an agent at New York, on "information and belief." Appeal from a decree of the District Court of the United States for the Southern District of New York respecting the British bark *Springbok* and her cargo, which had been captured at sea by the United States gunboat *Sonoma* during the late rebellion and libeled in the said court for prize.

The vessel was owned by May & Co., British subjects, and was commanded by James May, son of one of the owners.

She had been chartered 12th November, 1862, by authority of May, the captain, to T. S. Begbie, of London, to take a full cargo of "Lawful merchandise, and therewith *proceed to Nassau, or so near thereunto as she may safely get, and deliver same,* on being paid freight as follows &c., the freight to be paid one-half in advance on clearance from custom house, subject to insurance, and the remainder in cash *on delivery.* Bills of lading are to be signed by master at current rate of freight, if required, without prejudice to this charter party. It being agreed that master or owners have absolute lien on cargo for all freight, dead freight, demurrage, or other charges. The ship is to be consigned to the charter's agent at port of unloading, free of commission. Thirty running days are allowed the freighter for loading at port of loading and discharging at Nassau."

This document had an endorsement on it by Speyer & Haywood, persons hereinafter described.
The letter of instructions to the master was thus:

"LONDON, December 8, 1862

CAPTAIN JAMES MAY.
Dear Sir -- Your vessel being now loaded, you will proceed *at once to the port of Nassau, N.P., and on arrival report yourself to Mr. B. W. Hart there, who will give you orders as to the delivery of your cargo* and any further information you may require.
We are, dear sir &c.,
SPEYER & HAYWOOD,

For the Charters"

The letter to the agent of the consignee, directed "B. W. Hart, *Nassau,*" and from these same persons, Speyer & Heywood, was thus:

"*Under instructions from Messrs. Isaac, Campbell & Co.,* of Jermyn Street, we enclose you bills of lading for goods shipped per Springbok, consigned to you."

The London custom house certificate was "from London *to Nassau;*" the certificate of clearance declared the "destination of voyage, *Nassau, N.P.;*" and the manifest was of a cargo from "London *to Nassau.*"

The log book was headed, "Log book of the bark *Springbok* on a voyage from London *to Nassau.*"

The shipping articles, November, 1862, were of a British crew, "*on a voyage from London to Nassau, N.P.;* thence, if required, to any other port of the West India Islands, *American ports,* British North America, east coast of South America and back to the final port discharge in the United Kingdom or continent of Europe, between the Elbe and Brest, and finally to a port in the United Kingdom; voyage probably under twelve months."

The cargo, valued at £66,000, was covered by three bills of lading (of which two were duplicated, the duplicates marked Captain's copies), as follows:

Bill of lading market No. 2 showed "666 packages merchandise," shipped by Moses Brothers, to be delivered &c., at port of Nassau, N.P., unto order or to assigns, he or they paying freight, *as per charter party.* It was endorsed by Moses Brothers in blank. This bill of lading on its face showed 150 chests and 150 half-chests tea, 220 bags coffee, 4 cases ginger, 19 bags pimento, 10 bags cloves, and 60 bags pepper -- in all, 613 packages. The remaining 53 were entered as *cases, kegs,* and *casks.* These 53 packages were found, when the cargo was more closely examined, to contain *medicines* and *saltpetre,* matters at that time much needed in the Southern states, then under blockade. Bill of lading No. 3 showed one bale and one case shipped by Speyer & Haywood, to be delivered at Nassau unto order or to assigns &c., paying freight as per *charter party.*

Bill of lading No. 4 showed 1,339 packages shipped by Speyer & Haywood to Nassau, as above. These 1,339 packages were also described as *cases, bales, boxes,* and *a trunk.* This was also endorsed in blank.

The manifest gave no more specific description of the character of the cargo. It was signed Speyer & Haywood, brokers, and showed that the whole cargo was consigned to "order."

An examination of the packages in bills Nos. 3 and 4 showed 540 pairs of "gray army blankets," like those used in the army of the United States, and 24 pairs of "white blankets;" 360 gross of brass navy buttons, marked "C.S.N.," [Footnote 1] 10 gross of army buttons marked "A.," [Footnote 2]

397 gross of army buttons marked "I.," [Footnote 3] and 148 gross of army buttons marked "C.," [Footnote 4] being in all 555 gross; all the buttons were stamped on the under side "Isaac Campbell & Co., 71 Jermyn St., London." There were 8 cavalry sabres, having the British crown on their guards; 11 sword bayonets, 992 pairs of army boots, 97 pairs of russet brogans, and 47 pairs of cavalry boots &c.

The vessel set sail from London, December 8, 1862, and was captured February 3, 1863, making for the harbor of Nassau, in the British neutral island of New Providence and about 150 miles east of that place. The port, which lay not very far from a part of the southern coast of the United States, it was matter of common knowledge had been largely used as one for call and trans shipment of cargoes intended for the ports of the insurrectionary states of the Union, then under blockade by the Federal Government. [Footnote 5] The vessel when captured made no resistance, and all her papers were given up without attempt at concealment or spoilation.

Being brought into the port of New York and libeled there as prize, February 12, 1863, a claim was put in on the 9th of March following by Captain May for his father and others as owners of the vessel. On the 24th of the same month, a claim for the whole cargo was put in for Isaac, Campbell & Co., and also for Begbie through one Kursheet, their "agent and attorney;" Kursheet stating in his affidavit in behalf of these owners that "it is impossible to communicate with them *in time to allow them to make the claim and test affidavit herein.*" His affidavit stated farther, "That as he *is informed and believes,* it was not intended that the barque should attempt to enter any port of the United States or that her cargo should be delivered at any such port, but that the only destination of such cargo was Nassau aforesaid, where the said cargo was to *be actually disposed of and proceeds remitted to said claimants.*"

"That, as he *is informed and believes,* the cargo was not shipped in pursuance of any understanding either directly or indirectly, with any of the enemies of the United States or with any person or persons in behalf of or connected with the so called Confederate States of America, but was shipped with the full, fair, and honest intent to sell and dispose of the same absolutely in the market of Nassau aforesaid."

"That *his information is derived from letters and communications very lately received by this deponent from the aforesaid claimants,* and from documents in deponent's possession, placed there by said claimants, and that such communications *authorize this deponent to intervene and act as agent as well as proctor and advocate for the said claimants as to the above cargo.*" The master, mate, and steward, were examined as witnesses in preparatorio:

The master stated that the goods were to be delivered at Nassau for account and risk of Begbie & Co., London, the charterers; that he did not know that the laders or consignees had any interest in the goods; that he knew nothing of the qualities, quantities, or particulars of the goods or to whom they would belong if restored and delivered at the destined port; that he was not aware that there were goods contraband of war on board; that, as he believed, *invoices and duplicate bills of lading were sent to Nassau by mail steamer;* that there were no false bills of lading, nor any passports or sea-briefs other than the usual register and ship's papers, which were entirely true and fair; that *he did not know on what pretence she was captured;* that there were no persons on board owing allegiance to the United States; that on the vessel's previous voyage, she went from London to Jamaica, carrying general merchandise, and returned direct, carrying principally logwood.

The mate, who to a greater or less extent confirmed these statements, swore that the cargo was a general cargo -- casks, bales, boxes, and bags; that he had no knowledge, information, or belief as to what was contained in them, and had never heard. He knew of no goods contraband of war; no arms or munitions of war that he knew of. "The seizure," he stated, "was made on *the supposition that the cargo was contraband of war.*"
The boatswain testified to the same purpose of the voyage; that the vessel had no colors but English aboard; that the cargo was general, in bales, cases, and bags, that he did not know their contents and never had heard them stated, and that *he* "understood the seizure was made because the bills of lading *did not show what was in some of the cases on board.*" The steward, that he "understood the vessel was captured because *we had goods contraband of war aboard;* had heard no other reason given."

Upon the hearing in the district court, the counsel for the captors invoked into the case the proofs taken in two other cases, on the docket of that court for trial at the same time with the present one, the cases, namely, of *United*

States v. Steamer Gertrude and *United States v. Schooner Stephen Hart.* The *Hart* was captured on the 29th of January, 1862, between the southern coast of Florida and the Island of Cuba. The claimants of her whole cargo were the firm of Isaac, Campbell & Co., the same persons who claimed, jointly with Begbie, the cargo of the *Springbok.* It also appeared in the case of the *Hart* that the brokers who had charge of the lading of her cargo were Speyer & Haywood, the same parties who appeared as brokers of the cargo in the present case, and as shippers of a part of it, and as agents for Begbie and for I., C. & Co. It appeared in the case of the *Hart* that I., C. & Co. were dealers in military goods, and that the entire cargo of that vessel, consisting of arms, munitions of war, and military equipments, was laden on board of her in England under the direction of I., C. & Co., in cooperation with the agents, at London, of the "Confederate States" with the design that the cargo should run the blockade into a port of the enemy either in the *Hart* or in a vessel into which the cargo should be trans shipped at some place in Cuba, and that I., C. & Co. entrusted to the agent of the "Confederate States" in Cuba, the determination of the question as to the mode in which the cargo should be transported into the enemy's port. The cargo of the Hart had been condemned by the Supreme Court as lawful prize at the last term. U.S. [Footnote 6]

The Gertrude was captured on the 16th of April, 1863, in the Atlantic Ocean off one of the Bahama Islands while on a voyage ostensibly from Nassau to St. John's, N.B. The libel was filed against her on the 23rd of April, 1863, and she was condemned with her cargo as lawful prize on the 21st of July, 1863. No claim was put in to either the *Gertrude* or her cargo. The testimony showed that she belonged to Begbie; that her cargo consisted, among other things, of hops, dry goods, drugs, leather, cotton cards, paper, 3960 pairs of gray army blankets, 335 pairs of white blankets, linen, woollen shirts, flannel, 750 pairs of army brogans, Congress gaiters, and 24,900 pounds of powder; that she was captured after a chase of three hours, and when making for the harbor of Charleston, her master knowing of it blockade and having on board a Charleston pilot under an assumed name.

The marshal's report of the contents of the packages on board of the *Springbok* and of the prize commissioners' report of the contents of the packages of the *Gertrude* disclose the following facts:

The report in the case of the *Springbok* specified "18 bales of army blankets, butternut color," each marked *A, in a diamond,* and numbered 544 to 548, 550, 552, and 555 to 565. The report in the case of the *Gertrude* showed a large number of bales of "army blankets," each marked *A, in a diamond,* and numbered with numbers, scattered from 243 to 534, and then commencing to renumber again at 600.

In the cargo of the *Springbok* was found a bale marked *A, in a diamond,* and numbered 779; while in the cargo of the Gertrude were found bales each marked *A, in a diamond,* and numbered 780, 782, 784, 786, 788, 789 to 799. In the *Springbok* were found 9 cases, each marked *A, in a diamond,* and numbered 976 to 984, and 4 bales, each marked *A, in a diamond,* and numbered 985 to 987 and 989, by the same marks, the 4 bales being stated to be "men's colored traveling shirts." In the *Gertrude* were found 5 bales, each marked *A in a diamond* and numbered 998, 990, to 992 and 998, and described as "men's colored traveling shirts." In the *Hart* were 4 cases of men's white shirts, each marked *A in a diamond* and numbered 994 to 997.

So also, in the *Springbok* were found packages each marked *A, in a diamond, S. I., C. & Co.,* and numbered irregularly and with considerable *hiatus,* from 1221 up to 1440. But there was no 1285 among them, the *hiatus* being from 1266 to 1289, which last was the first of several having "shirts." On the *Gertrude* were packages marked *A, in a diamond,* numbered from 1170 to 1214, also one numbered 1285, and found to contain "shirts."

On board of the *Springbok* was found 1 bale of brown wrapping paper, marked *A, in a diamond, T. S. & Co.* and numbered 264. On board of the *Gertrude* a large number of bales of wrapping paper and other paper marked *A, in a diamond, T. S. & CO.* and numbered with numbers scattered between 1 and 170.

In only one instance, apparently, so far as the testimony showed, was the same number found on a package in each cargo. On the other hand, many marks were found on the one vessel not found on the other. No application was made in the court below for leave to furnish further proofs. The court below condemned both vessel and cargo.

APPENDIX G

Northampton Shoe Factory

Northampton Shoe Factory 1869 (1)

"...We see shoemakers and shoemakeresses at work in dingy ground-floor rooms and at open upper windows; he notices "Riveters' Entrance", & c., painted on the finger-rubbed doors of the many-windowed factories which might be taken for little cotton mills (metal rivets were used in cheaper kinds of footwear to attach soles to uppers and insoles).

Let us go to Messrs. Turner Brothers (Hyde & Co)... in Campbell Square. The first impression produced us one of the queer contrasts that there are in the cordwainer's trade. The cobbler, cramped in his cupboard-like stall, belongs to it, and so does the firm, which employs four hundred hands on, and four times as many off, the premises. In one long room, five rows of clickers, with pale faces and dirty aprons with a pent-house or brief upper skirt of leather at the waist, are cutting on wooden slabs, and blocks like butchers', all kinds of women's materials; in another tougher men's materials are being manipulated. When cut, the uppers are rolled up, placed in ticketed baskets, and sent up to the operatives in other parts of the premises, or away to outside hands. A boot or shoe often goes out in this way twice before it is finished, and stacked in the drying-room heated by steam pipes. Down below there is a puff of steam; wheels whir, bands run round and round, machinery clanks. Soles and heels and "split-lifts" [split-lift - narrow strip of leather wedge-shaped in section, curved so that it forms a marginal heel layer] are being punched out by iron frames that come down upon the leather with a thud, and when punched, slide down shoots into the bin-like receptacles beneath. These lads are pricking holes for the riveters by the aid of a machine; that old man is passing leather, to harden it, between steam-turned rollers. It is curious to note the difference between hand work and machine work. Close by a sole-cutting machine a young man or two are cutting up odds and ends of leather into soles by hand. Although they have the aid of the machinery to press the leather into shape, it is almost ludicrous to remark how few they make in comparison to the machine. Soles and heels are garnered in great pigeon holes. Shaped leather of all sorts is arranged on shelves in ticketed baskets. Cistern-like tin-lined cases, inner lined with brown paper, are gaping for their loads. Here is a pile of boots done up in pairs in white and green tissue paper; there is a pyramid of bright pink boxes, each holding a dozen pairs. Here the patent-leather tops of boots for South American gallopers over the Pampas are being eyeleted. Specially gay and graceful are the women's boots intended for Spanish-American countries; sky blue, with a golden star on the instep; mauve, golden-bronze, like a butterfly's wing, green, with a sheen like a drake's neck; pink, yellow, and black, with coquettish little ankle tassels. Close by are shoes for New Zealand servant girls that looked as if their wearers would never need a second pair; and not far off, as substantial seeming sea boots for Newfoundland cod fishers. In an adjoining room there is an "infinite variety" a dazzling variety of many-coloured babies' shoes, varying in price from 5d. up to 30s.

"And what is the value of Northampton's export of shoes?"
"A million sterling per annum would be a low estimate" is the answer.
"And what are the average wages of the hands?" "Oh, it is almost impossible to strike an average. Some of mine a very few make £3 per week; more make £2; but I dare say a good many do not make more than 12s. It depends entirely on the man himself."

A large proportion of the Northampton shoemakers struck me, during my recent visit to them, as being decided members of the alcoholic persuasion. I met them mooning about, unshorn, unkempt, - a condition in which too many of them remain in the day on which they need not work with filmy eyes which showed that they had gone on the "fuddle". I met them staggering. I saw them sparring one with his apron down, and the other with his apron hastily rolled up around his waist and then suddenly knocking off knocking each other, and amicably nodding their heads together, as if they had quite forgotten that they had been trying to blacken each other's eyes

two seconds before. It is, I am informed, "the thing" with the Northampton shoemaker to take what he calls a "Sunday-Monday": Id est, he works on Sunday, that he may have the more to lush on Monday.
(1) Rove, Richard, *Northampton in 1869*, (abridged) Good Words Magazine, November 1869

APPENDIX H

A contradiction with nothing to contradict

THE LONDON TIMES JULY 10th 1858

A Contradiction With Nothing To Contradict.

"TO THE EDITOR OF THE LONDON TIMES ILLUSTRATED.

Dear Sir,
In your publication of Thursday there appeared, under the heading of "Military and Naval Intelligence," a paragraph directly reflecting upon our firm, and which is a tissue of misrepresentations. We therefore appeal to your impartiality to insert our reply. We have supplied the equivalent of upwards of 30,000 soldiers' kits to the Government depot at Weedon; the contract price was 21. Ils. 10d. There being 32 articles in a kit, the supply of each article was sent in as it could be manufactured, separately, and they were separately examined, the rejections being but 13 per cent. We deny that anything like this proportion should have been rejected, and it is in evidence before the Committee upon Government Contracts that the inspector was an unfortunate farmer, and wholly unfit for the duty which he assumed; and it is also in evidence that the rejections were made by "rule of thumb," or, in other words, without actual inspection. Our arrangements with our manufacturers were that the goods were to be equal to the sample pattern of the War Office, and that if they were not, they were not to charge them to our account. When we found that a considerable number of the rejections had been unjustly made, and that the goods were really equal to pattern, we could not in fairness throw those returned to us upon the hands of our manufacturers; and,

I receiving orders from colonels of regiments for kits, which the Government establishment was unable to furnish, we sent them some of the articles which had been rejected at Weedon. The supplies so made were examined at each regiment and depot by a regimental board, compared with the official pattern, and passed. The quality is therefore a moot point. The farmer at Weedon says it was inferior to pattern; the regimental boards say it was equal, we assert that it is superior. At all events, they have been approved by gentlemen well conversant with the wear and tear of all the articles supplied (none having been returned) and we have been paid for them by the Government. Our charge for the kits we supplied directly to regiments was considerably higher than the contract price at which we had sent them to Weedon, but considerably under the statement of your informant. When we tendered for the original contract we unfortunately miscalculated the cost to ourselves. The highest tender sent in was about £3. 7s. 6d., the lowest, independently of our own, was about £3, and our contract price was £2. 11s. 10 1d. Being the lowest, we were successful at a loss of £12,000. The principal member of our firm is still under examination by the Contracts Committee upon this subject; but I could not refrain from making this explanation in reply to your unprovoked and erroneous attack on our house.

We are, Sir, your obedient servants,

S ISAAC CAMPBELL & CO. 21, St. James Street, Pall-Mall,
JULY 9th 1858.

As requested, we publish this letter from Messrs. Isaac Campbell and Co., of 21, St. James Street. As a fitting illustration of it, we also reprint the extract from our Naval and Military intelligence which has called forth this letter, and which they characterize as "a tissue of misrepresentations".

"It appears that one of the largest army contractors to supply soldiers' kits at 21s. 6d each, and his contract been accepted, several thousand kits were sent into the clothing stores at Weedon, when it was discovered that the articles supplied were of an inferior description, and not worth the sum paid for them by the Government. On this discovery being made the kits were returned to the contractor, who has since supplied some kits to the troops at Chatham for £3 8s 9d each. It appears that articles which were rejected by the Government as not being worth £2 11s 3d. at Weedon are considered to be worth £3 8s 9d.

at Chatham, and are purchased by the Government for the troops at that price. Since the authorities have agreed to present each recruit with a free kit, the whole expense of the soldiers' necessaries borne by the Government, instead of being charged to the recruit as here to fore. Having done this, we will leave it to the common sense of the reader to decide whether every allegation of our correspondent is not distinctly admitted by the firm. The kits were rejected at Weedon, and the rejected kits were then forwarded for the use of the troops at Chatham at an advanced price. This is what our correspondent asserted, and Messrs S. Isaac, Campbell & Co today endorse the statement. They put, of course, their own interpretation on the transaction, but that just now is the point in dispute."

APPENDIX I

OBITUARIES

SAMUEL ISAAC OBITUARY

Jewish Chronicle 26th November, 1886, p10

"Major Samuel Isaac". We regret to announce the death of Major Samuel Isaac, the Lesseps* of the Mersey Tunnel, who expired on Monday afternoon at his residence in Warrington Crescent, Maida Vale, at the age of 74. Major Isaac was born in Chatham, came to London as a young man, and carried on a large business as an army contractor in Jermyn Street, under the firm of Isaac, Campbell & Co, his brother, Mr Saul Isaac, JP, formerly Member of Parliament for Nottingham, being another member of the partnership. The firm were during the Confederate War in America the largest European supporters of the Southern states and their ships laden with military stores and freighted home with cotton, were the most enterprising of the blockade runners. The late Major Isaac's eldest son, Mr Henry Isaac, who died at Nassau, West Indies, during the war had much to do with this branch of the work. Major Isaac's military rank was conferred on him in connection with his services in raising a regiment of volunteers from among the workmen at his own factory in Northampton. Messrs Isaac, Campbell & Co were naturally large holders of Confederate bonds. The commercial house fell shortly after the fall of the Confederacy and Major Isaac's enormous mansion at Kensington, tenanted after him for a season by the Begum of Oudh, long stood vacant. He was not, however, the man to be daunted by failure. After a time he acquired the rights of the promoters of the Mersey Railway – a project which had obtained the sanction of Parliament, but had remained dormant owing to the disinclination of capitalists to venture on the heroic task of tunnelling the bed of the Mersey. With unfailing courage and persistence Major Isaac pushed the scheme into practical development. He himself undertook to make the tunnel, letting the works to Messrs Waddell, and seeking the invaluable assistance as engineers of Brunlees and Sir Douglas Fox. Fresh powers were obtained from Parliament, money was raised in bonds and shares, and the tunnel was duly opened under the auspices of the Prince of Wales. His first wife was Miss Symonds of Dover, by whom he had three children. He married secondly Emma, daughter of the late Stephen Hart, of Haydon Square, London, who survives him, as does their daughter Mrs Arnold Crombach, with other issue. The funeral was solemnised yesterday (Thursday) at the Willesden Cemetery of the United Synagogue."

* Lesseps was the French designer of the Suez canal

SAUL ISAAC OBITUARY

Jewish Chronicle 9th October, 1903.

Mr Saul Isaac MP for Nottingham from 1874 to 1880, died on Tuesday at 109 Greencroft Gardens, South Hampstead, and he is to be buried today at Willesden, the funeral leaving the house at 12 o'clock. He had a chequered and romantic career. He was born eighty years ago, and his early years were passed at Chatham, where his family were engaged in the furniture business. The experience of military requirements gained in this important garrison enabled elder brother, the late Major Samuel Isaac, and himself, to become at a later period the principal army contractors and European agents of the Confederate Government in the struggle between Northern and Southern States of the great American Republic. Their firm at this date was Campbell, Isaac &Co., of Jermyn Street, and their business was to run the blockade which the more powerful fleet of the Federals maintained against the Confederates. Mr Saul Isaac's nephew, Henry, a daring and handsome young man, went out to Nassau, West Indies, to superintend these operations, and died there of yellow fever. The liabilities of the Confederates were paid in bonds, and when the defeat of the South became definitive, Mr Isaac's firm was the largest holder of these bonds. With the fall of the Confederation, its principal European commercial supporters fell also. A remarkable fact was the subsequent financial recovery of both partners. They had married sisters, the misses Hart, ladies who had inherited substantial separate estate, and after resigning their mercantile assets and their well appointed private establishments to their creditors, the brothers had still from their wives' means the opportunity of starting again. The elder brother became the maker of the Mersey tunnel, and thus acquired a second fortune, though ultimately he left his affairs considerably involved. The younger brother, the subject of his memoir, became the owner of Clifton collieries at Nottingham. Shortly afterwards he was elected for the important borough (now city) near which his collieries were situated; and he was bidden to Windsor by the sovereign. In those days, Jewish emancipation being comparatively recent, the Jewish members were all Liberals, and Mr Isaac was the first Jew to take a seat on the Conservative side, the first Jewish Member of Parliament to support Lord Beaconsfield, the first Jew elected a member of the Carlton Club. He was a handsome young man of good presence, but speculative and unstable in his business affairs, and his second period of brilliance proved as fleeting as the first. He fell into difficulties from which he is believed never to have recovered. Mr Isaac was married twice and leaves issue. Mr Isaac continued to take interest in Jewish matters, and write to us as recently as 13th August, 1902 in reference to what he was good enough to call "our very able article" on "Some events in the days of the King".

CALEB HUSE OBITUARY

New York Times March 13th, 1905

Col Caleb Huse Dead.

Northerner was South's Purchasing Agent During Civil War.

HIGHLAND FALLS, N. Y, March 12.
Col Caleb Huse, aged seventy-five years, died suddenly at his home here today, following a surgical operation. Col. Huse was graduated from the United States Military Academy in 1851, and for many years was an instructor at West Point.
He resigned from the Union Army in 1861, and subsequently was commissioned by Jefferson Davis as Colonel and sent to Europe as purchasing agent for the Confederate Army. He remained abroad in that capacity until

the end of hostilities. For a year prior to the war of the rebellion he was Superintendent and Commandant of Cadets in the University of Alabama. Col. Huse was born at Newburyport, Mass. He is survived by his wife, three sons, and five daughters. One son, Harry J P Huse is a Professor of Mathematics at the Naval Academy

APPENDIX J

Accoutrement invoice

A PHOTOGRAPH OF AN S. ISAAC, CAMPBELL & CO INVOICE FOR ACCOUTREMENTS FOR THE CONFEDERATE GOVERNMENT
(Courtesy of the South Carolina Confederate Relic Room and Museum)

APPENDIX K

Greatcoat invoice

A PHOTOGRAPH OF AN S. ISAAC, CAMPBELL & CO INVOICE FOR GREATCOATS FOR THE CONFEDERATE GOVERNMENT
(Courtesy of the South Carolina Confederate Relic Room and Museum)

BIOGRAPHIES

David Charles Burt and Craig Lee Barry are from opposite sides of the Atlantic. They both became interested in how British companies supplied the Confederacy during the American Civil War. Separately, they started to research the firms involved, the arms, equipage and uniforms supplied by these companies.

David published his first book, *Major Caleb Huse C.S.A. & S Isaac Campbell & Co* in March 2009. It reached No 1 on the online retailer Amazon UK history charts. After its publication, David and Craig, author of *The Civil War Musket: A Handbook for Historical Accuracy – Lock, Stock and Barrel* and Editor of the *Watchdog*, got together to write their first title, *The Civil War Musket: J.E. Barnett & Sons*.

Supplier to the Confederacy: S, Isaac Campbell & Co, London is the revised and expanded second edition of David's first book. This is the second book the pair have written together. The third, *Supplier to the Confederacy: Peter Tait & Co, Limerick*, is nearing completion.

David lives in Congleton, Cheshire, England. Craig lives in Murfreesboro, Tennessee, U.S.A.